EUROPE

ASIA

Lisbon

AFRICA

ATLANTIC OCEAN

Mozambique
Island

Site of
Shipwreck

Cape Town

D1474491

FROM NO
RETURN

FROM NO RETURN

The 221-Year Journey of the Slave Ship São José

1794

Jaco Jacqes Boshoff

Lonnie G. Bunch III

Paul Gardullo

Stephen C. Lubkemann

Smithsonian
*National Museum of African American
History and Culture*

*Clifton,
Table Bay, ca. 2014*

Published by Smithsonian Enterprises
on behalf of the Smithsonian Institution
and the National Museum of African American History and Culture

Distributed by Smithsonian Books

600 Maryland Avenue SW Suite 6001
Washington, DC 20024 USA

www.si.edu   nmaahc.si.edu

Smithsonian

21 20 19 18 17   6 5 4 3 2

ISBN 978-1-58834-606-3

Manufactured in Canada

All income from our sales supports the chartered educational purposes and
activities of the Smithsonian Institution.

Illustration, Document and Photography Credits on page 106

For the 512 aboard the São José

who are no longer forgotten

———————◆———————

and for the many millions more

ATLANTIC OCEA

Caribbean Islands

SOUTH AMERICA

The Global Slave Trade

Origins of enslaved Africans estimated by region, 1501-1867

The Middle Passage
CAPTIVES AS COMMODITIES

The transatlantic voyage between Africa and the Americas that created the African diaspora, in which millions of captive Africans were brought to the New World as slaves, was called the Middle Passage. The voyage was the second, or middle, part of a three-part journey that made up the Triangle Trade. Commodities from Europe, such as gunpowder, were shipped to Africa in exchange for captive human cargo. The captives were then exchanged in the Americas for sugar and tobacco, which were shipped to Europe. The enslaved Africans aboard the São José were the essential middle part of this equation: the human cargo.

EUROPE

AMERICA

AFRICA

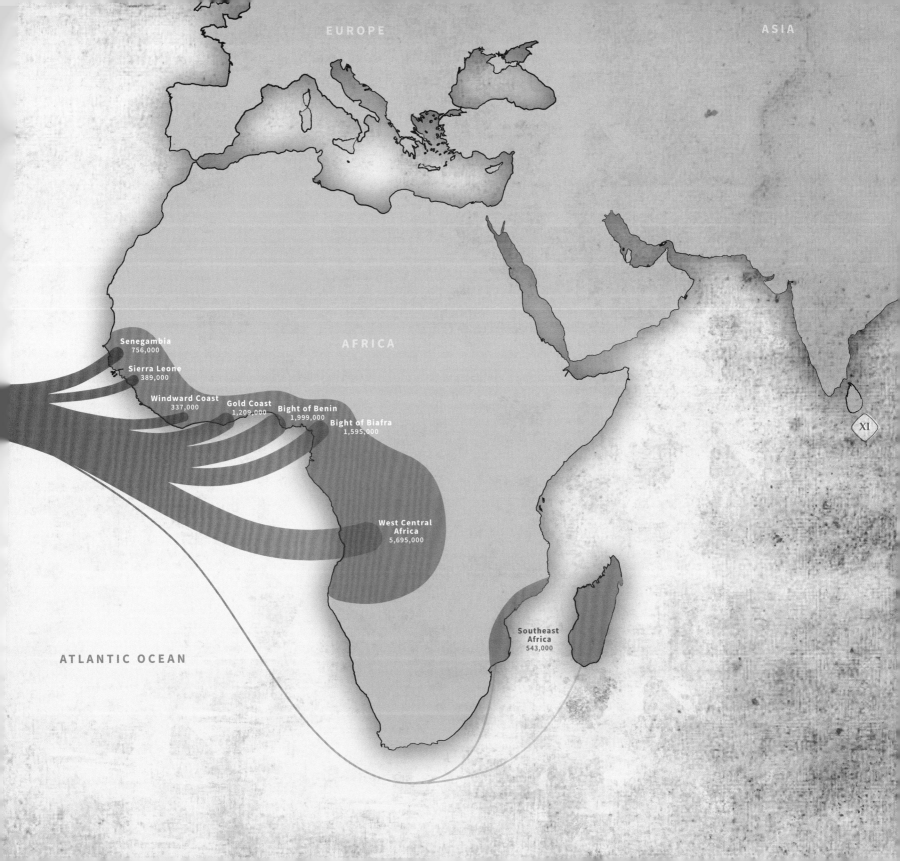

EUROPE

ASIA

AFRICA

Senegambia
756,000

Sierra Leone
389,000

Windward Coast
337,000

Gold Coast
1,209,000

Bight of Benin
1,999,000

Bight of Biafra
1,595,000

West Central
Africa
5,695,000

Southeast
Africa
543,000

ATLANTIC OCEAN

XI

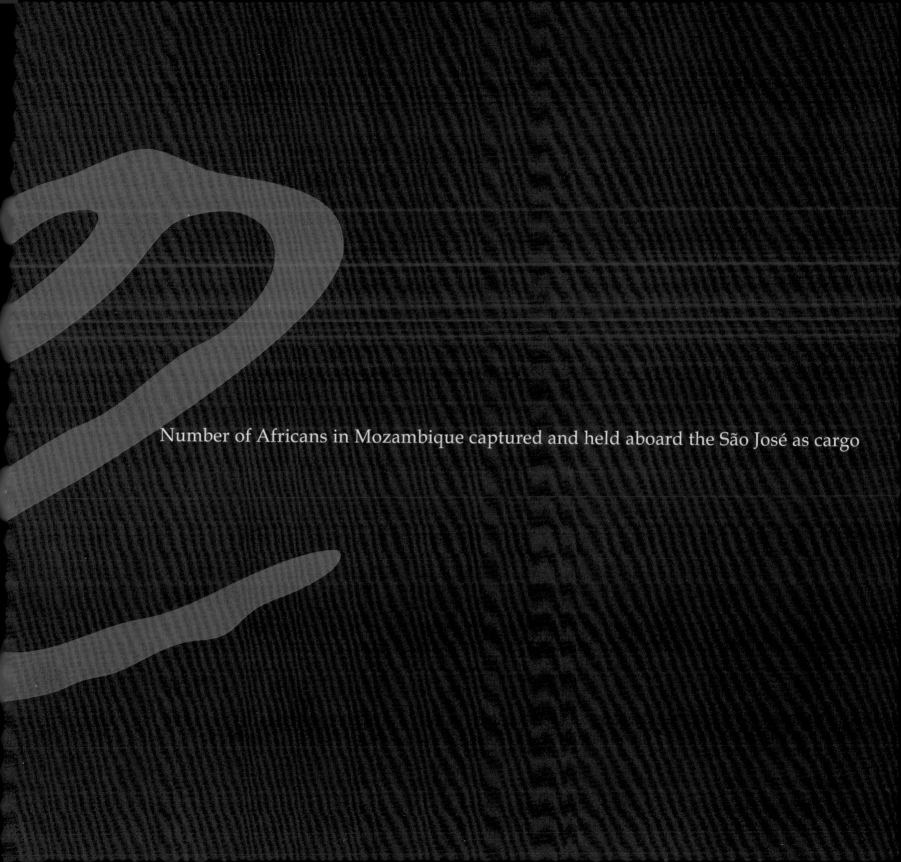

Number of Africans in Mozambique captured and held aboard the São José as cargo

Paul Gardullo

DECEMBER

The last week in December of each year marks the anniversary of the final days of the voyage of the Portuguese slave ship *São José Paquete d'Africa*. Carrying more than five hundred captive Mozambicans from their home and bound for Maranhão, Brazil, the ship was caught in storms and swells off the coast of Cape Town in South Africa near the Cape of Good Hope, where it foundered and wrecked. Battered on the punishing coastline for more than two hundred years, the remnants of that ship are humble and few: small pieces of timber, concretized shackles, copper fastenings, a pulley block that would have been used to hoist a sail, several cannons and cannonballs, and a number of the more than eleven hundred iron bars of ballast on board that the ship's crew used to counterbalance the weight of the cargo of human lives.

Left: Iron ballast blocks
Right: Cannonball

The site of one of the first successful efforts worldwide to document the archaeological vestiges of the Middle Passage, this single ship has come to symbolize the many thousands of vessels that trafficked in human lives in the transatlantic and African slave trades. Through the actions of an innovative global collaboration intent on recovering not just the history of this voyage but also those small remnants of the vessel, we are able to begin to reclaim the stories, lives, and souls of those five hundred and twelve Mozambicans, half of whom perished in the waves, the other half of whom were saved, only to be sold back into slavery in the western cape of South Africa.

This book is a meditation on, a journey into, and a commemoration of those lives at one moment in time two hundred twenty-one years after its voyage. It is a demonstration of a new model of research and public engagement that helps all people relate to and more deeply understand the slave trade and its enduring legacies. And it is a celebration of the transformative power and potential of bringing this story back into the shared memory of individuals, communities, and nations across the globe.

LEGACIES

The slave trade was a massive endeavor with a global reach. For more than four hundred years beginning in the fifteenth century, at least twelve million Africans were captured, forced to leave their homelands and loved ones, trafficked, and dispersed throughout the Atlantic world. The modern world cannot be understood without tracing the geographic, economic, political, cultural, and psychological routes of dislocation, relocation, and loss of this largest forced migration in human history that resulted in the African diaspora.

At once a history of colonialism and capitalism, of oppression and violence, and of economics and religion, the massive, overwhelming scale of this trade, whose prime commodity was human beings, can be difficult to grasp. Profits from the sale of enslaved humans and their labor laid the economic foundation for Western Europe, the Caribbean, and the Americas, helping to create the nation-states of Portugal, Spain, the Netherlands, France, Great Britain, and the United States, as well as others in Europe, the Caribbean, and South America. The Church, along with merchants, families, and individuals, benefited from these profits, which also helped build the assets of banks, insurance companies, and other institutions, some of which are still with us today.

Right: Table of ships, payments, and commodities, including enslaved captives, from Africa to Rio de Janeiro, Bahia, and Pernambuco in Brazil, between 1789 and 1793.

Far Right: Document with table of voyages in 1794 between Benguela, Angola, in southwestern Africa and Rio de Janeiro, Brazil, detailing the traffic of ivory, slaves, and other commodities. Dated Benguela, 20 January 1795, one month after the voyage of the São José from Mozambique.

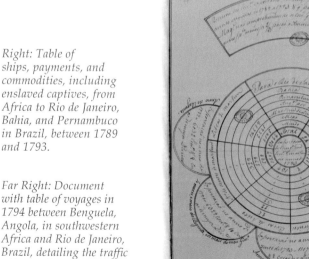

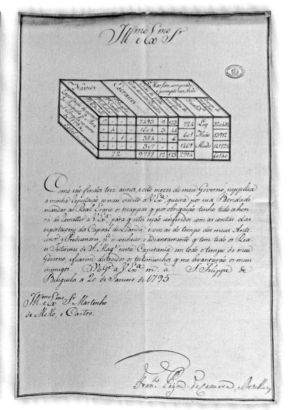

Meditation

Set in balance with this tremendous development of wealth was its immense human cost—the physical and psychological toll on the enslaved and the deep impoverishment of Africa. For far too many of us, the intimacy of individual lives are lost among or abstracted in the numbers. But they were, in the words of my curatorial colleagues Nancy Bercaw, Mary Elliot, and Tsione Wolde-Michael, "inscribed in every coin that changed hands, each spoonful of sugar stirred into a cup of tea, each puff of a pipe, and every bite of rice" across this long arc of history.

The story of the São José is a singular moment within that arc. It reclaims the human scale and provides a tangible reference for us to grapple with the trade and its legacies in Africa, Europe, and the Americas. Perhaps the single greatest symbol of the trade is the ships that carried captive Africans across the Atlantic, with those who survived the journey never to return. In Europe and the Americas, governments, businesses, and entrepreneurs built and retrofitted vessels to meet the ever-growing demand for enslaved Africans. Adorned with flags of their countries as well as with banners of the merchant companies that held monopolies to trade in human capital, slavers came in many different sizes and forms across the centuries, depending on the needs, demands, and acceptability of the trade. No more than a handful, however, have been archaeologically documented, and none during the slaving leg of a journey. That is the uniqueness of the São José.

During the eighteenth century, the end of which saw the doubly tragic voyage of the São José, the slave trade peaked, trafficking more than 7.2 million Africans to the Americas. In a time that marked the Age of Enlightenment, an era of revolutions—American, French, Haitian—burgeoning democracy, and the

birth of the abolitionist movement, it was common for at least thirty slave ships to sit at anchor off the ports of the West African coast at a single time, awaiting human cargo to be transported from shore. The Portuguese began to reorient trade from its colony of Mozambique, which had been associated with trade throughout East Africa and the Indian Ocean for nearly a millennium, to the wider transatlantic slave trade that had long centered along West Africa. After several stops along the coast, ships from West and East Africa, their hulls packed to capacity, were ready to set sail across the Atlantic. Named with cruel irony after saints, saviors, martyrs, and ideals such as benevolence, prosperity, and salvation, these ships were more aptly labeled much later by the historian Marcus Rediker as "floating dungeons."

Our understanding of what happened during these execrable months-long voyages aboard these vessels is slim. It exists primarily in the written record—relegated to the few written testimonies of those who survived the voyages and later escaped bondage, to the words of captains or crew or free observers aboard or ashore, to the cold calculation of ledger books and other materials from the archival record of this very meticulously managed trade. What we do know is that enslaved Africans were kept in appalling conditions. Slave traders loaded their ships with care for humans only as commodities. Some packed enslaved people together as tightly as possible, counting on the larger number to make up for the loss of life, and profit, on the voyage. Others compressed their human cargo less, hoping that more people would survive and yield more profit at the journey's end.

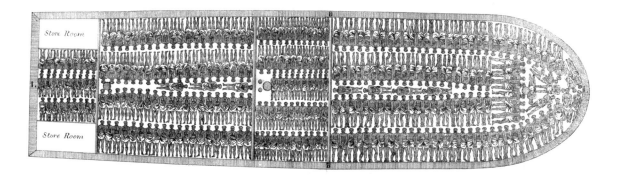

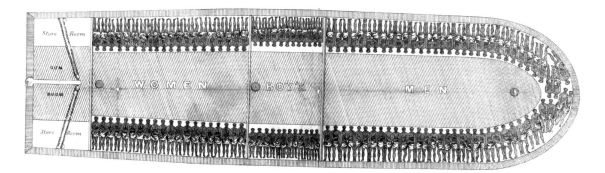

Men, women, and children were loaded in the hulls of ships, often chained two-by-two, in tight spaces that made sitting or standing impossible. Women were often subject to rape by their captors, and all faced the risk of disease. The sick or deceased were thrown overboard to the sharks that regularly followed behind. Despite these conditions, enslaved people were not quiet victims. They rebelled on one in ten voyages; and rather than endure the horrors of enslavement, accounts record that many also sought freedom by jumping overboard. "The shrieks of the women, and the groans of the dying, rendered the whole a scene of horror almost inconceivable," wrote the Nigerian Olaudah Equiano in his 1789 autobiography. Captured and enslaved, he eventually was able to gain his freedom, and was one of the few such survivors able to read and write English. While many souls were lost during the Middle Passage, those who survived, like Equiano, did so through courage, strength,

Above: Detail from the illustration of the Brookes slave ship, 1788

Meditation

and the will of the human spirit—but at great cost. Another elderly enslaved man stated that "the iron entered into our souls," as he described the shackles that dug into and tore more than just his flesh. But while testimonies from those named and unnamed provide crucial historical evidence, there is vast silence in the record overall, and the picture will remain forever incomplete without delving more deeply into other sources of evidence beyond the archive. In many ways, maritime archaeology is one of those last untapped resources that will enhance our understanding of slavery.

HISTORY VISIBLE

A worldwide initiative begun in 2008 is helping to fill this silence. The Slave Wrecks Project is an international network of collaborators whose mission is to help uncover these submerged stories, to begin to build and share knowledge about a part of history that has been considered unknowable, and to find ways for individuals and communities to come to terms with these difficult histories. Along with the National Museum of African American History and Culture, as the Project's host, core project partners such as Iziko Museums of South Africa, The George Washington University, the U.S. National Park Service, Diving With a Purpose, the African Centre for Heritage Activities, and

Above: Concretized shackle

others bring together complementary strengths and capacities to mount international efforts with communities, in archives, within museums, on coastlines, and in the water.

Our journey begins, but doesn't end, with the São José. The Slave Wrecks Project is engaged in discovering and bringing back into memory the stories of other voyages and histories, and their own unique trajectories of the slave trade, with its variety of partners in the Caribbean, West Africa, South and North America. In a growing list of locations from Mozambique to South Africa to St. Croix, Senegal, Brazil, and Cuba, the project is generating new scholarship on the study of the global slave trade, particularly through the lens of slave shipwrecks. The focus is on ships and their voyages, because they provide windows for us into specific historical and cultural landscapes in Africa, Europe, and the Americas that are directly linked by trajectories of the trade. Just as important, learning from this precious and overlooked heritage can bring people face to face with authentic tangible pieces from that past, providing an experience and an immediacy unrecorded in archives, unmatched in words, and unplumbed by statistics.

The most powerful part of this project, however, is how it seeks to look to the present and to the future to find relevance and connections, and to bring understanding and healing to people in different countries and locales. Tying rigorous research and discovery directly together with education and training, we are empowering a new generation of African and African American maritime archaeologists and helping to make these histories visible for people well outside traditional venues. Working with cultural and historical institutions, we are creating novel mechanisms for linking to heritage tourism, to both preserve and protect the overlooked and endangered heritage of sites related to the slave trade. With its international scope, its spirit of collaboration, discovery, and education, and its goal to change institutions and lives, the Slave Wrecks Project engages with a difficult past to craft a promising future, bringing these discoveries not just to the museum on America's National Mall, but to other sites and institutions around the globe, to raise consciousness about this fundamental chapter in history that continues to shape our world.

CROSSROADS

The voyage of the Saõ José in the late eighteenth century was one of exploitation, subjugation, and slavery. We are dedicated to making the process of the recovery of this tragic history in the early twenty-first century one of repair, openness, and cooperation amongst individuals, institutions, communities, and nations. In confronting this dark past and helping people to better conceive of it, we hope to both understand our world and forge a better future amidst the wreckage of this shared heritage. Information and collaboration are now flowing along the routes that once carried slave ships, adding new international voices and perspectives to one story within the slave trade. Our work on Mozambique Island, in Cape Town, in northeast Brazil, in Washington, and on other points demarcated by the trajectory of the São José is catalyzing conversations amongst the communities of people who lay claim to its legacy. All are coming to realize that part of their history may involve connections to and conversations with people that are half a world away but who share a common

theme and a common story—one that started with the investigation of a single shipwreck.

We think of our work as existing on a crossroads—one between researchers and communities, between cultures and nations, the past and the present, ancestors and descendants, and between the sea and the land, bringing what is submerged above the horizon line, back into memory for all to see. On Mozambique Island, bringing the story into memory may have practical and positive implications for battling treasure hunting that endangers vital cultural heritage of the region. In the village of Mossuril in northern Mozambique, bringing the São José into memory means forging ties to and providing closure for communities whose ancestors were lost and now symbolically found on a beach in Cape Town. For the community of Clifton, most adjacent to the wreck, bringing the story into memory means never forgetting the history that lies offshore, caring for and protecting its legacy, knowing the deep connections that others around the world have to it.

Bringing this story into memory in the wider western cape of South Africa may mean acknowledging a longer and deeper presence of Mozambican identity in the region, and may help to inform current debates about xenophobia, national identity, and slavery's history there. In Portugal, it may mean ushering in a long overdue reckoning with the historic role of slavery and slave trading in the consciousness of this proud seafaring nation. In Maranhão, Brazil, bringing the story into memory means potentially finding connections back to villages in Mozambique, where subsequent slaving voyages brought captives who survived enslavement and whose descendent communities exist today. Finally, bringing this story into memory in the United

13

States means a deep acknowledgment of the global scope of slavery and the way in which all of us who are Americans must face our abiding connections to that not-so-distant past.

SPIRITS

Each of us who works with the Slave Wrecks Project also shares profound experiences on this complex crossroads. My crossroads moment came during my first time on the wreck site itself. I had long heard about the enormous challenges that the site presented to diving and working, but on this particular day in March 2014, the weather was sunny and warm and the sea unusually calm. Jaco Boshoff and his team ushered me out to the site, where I dipped below the surface into the cold, murky water. Following Jaco closely, seeking with his guidance, I received a tour of the few aspects of the wreck that could be seen above the sand—fragments, really: one of the cannons, a timber wedged beneath two large boulders— and began to discern a few features of what would only later become clear. We were there to carefully retrieve the São José's pulley block, a small but integral part of the ship's rigging, that would have been used to hoist sails, or perhaps lift barrels of cargo. In Jaco's parlance, it was akin to the ship's engine.

As an observer, I hovered slightly above, watching the team labor to do the final documentation and prepare to remove the piece from the place where it had rested so long. I thought about what my friend Kamau Sadiki, one of our partners from the Diving With a Purpose team, had related to me when he first dived the site—that upon touching a timber he felt as if he could feel the souls of those who had died there. From that moment, he told me, he knew he had to work on the São José. I was coming to a similar understanding about the power of this place firsthand. I thought about my initial conversations with Lonnie Bunch, my director, when tasked with the project, and some of the reservations I'd had about the ability and even the importance of finding the remnants of a slave ship, and his reassurances to trust that things would become clear. I remembered my first meeting with Steve Lubkemann and how, in learning about this expansive project that I immediately sensed was about much more than merely a single ship, it had the potential to effect real change in the world in the ways that I understood were rooted in the very mission and purpose of my museum.

I mostly marveled, however, at the beauty of the day, and the unusual calmness of this so often angry spot in the sea. I watched as the team gingerly began to remove the wooden block from place. At that moment, a strong surge suddenly and forcefully coursed through the entire area, pushing all of the divers several feet forward and then back, unmoored from all things solid and attached to the seafloor. In the next moment the pulley block came free and the surge passed. It was as if, alarmed for a moment, the sea just as quickly calmed, settled, and grew peaceful with the work taking place. I couldn't help but feel as if the spirits of ancestors were close by.

TOUCHSTONES

What we choose to save, recover, hold up to the light of day and remember are crucial—personally and collectively, unofficially and officially, for the body politic and for the human soul. The physical remnants of the São José are fragile

and incomplete — wrecked fragments long buried below the sand and surge of a forbidding coastline. Fragile though they are, these items, so long submerged both literally and metaphorically, contain extraordinary power for reflection, knowledge, and repair. Through them we are refashioning our connections to the past and our conversations with ourselves and each other, as Americans and global citizens.

These touchstones, and objects like them, are almost all of what we have to access and understand this past, to reflect upon and grapple with a trade that spanned the globe and shaped world history, and through which millions tragically lost their lives and millions more struggled with unimaginable resolve to survive and keep themselves whole. Seen through this lens, these castaway objects take on the most important meanings and become the foundational blocks of a project, a collaboration, and of an institution seeking to plumb and produce a fuller understanding of American and world history.

Like the iron ballast recovered from the São José, these items again measure the weight of human lives and the weight of human history. It is our job to grapple with that weight. To again hold it and to calculate it according to our own moral compass. Not as slave traders and traffickers did, but to a new calibration — one based on making the mute iron speak to the spirits and souls of those lives lost.

For hundreds of years, the slave ship was a vessel used for dehumanization and degradation. It is our duty as a vessel of change in the twenty-first century to engage with and expand that history, making our work for a better future a transformative force in the world as natural as living and breathing.

Pulley block

Meditation

Some other time, man or woman, traveler,

later, when I am not alive,

look here, look for me

between stone and ocean,

in the light storming

through the foam.

Look here, look for me,

for here I will return, without saying a thing,

without voice, without mouth, pure,

here I will return to be the churning

of the water, of

its unbroken heart,

here, I will be discovered and lost:

here, I will, perhaps, be stone and silence.

"I Will Return," Pablo Neruda

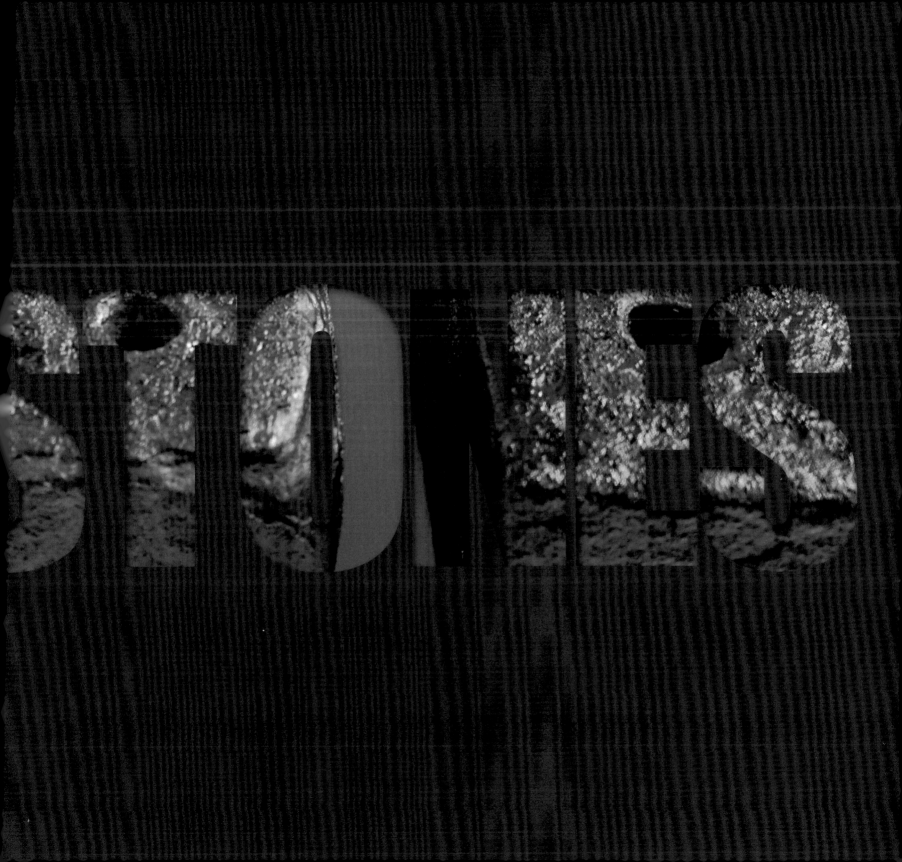

Number of captured Africans who perished as a result of the December 27, 1794 shipwreck

Stephen C. Lubkemann and Jaco Jacqes Boshoff

DISCOVERY 2004

We launched the Slave Wrecks Project with a search for four shipwrecks, all hailing from the high mark of the slave trade in the second half of the eighteenth century: Le Jardinière, La Cybele, the Meermin, and the São José. The captain of Le Jardinière was a cause célèbre in his own day—ensuring his vessel's maritime misfortune had been publicized and his work as an explorer and a botanist well remembered, even if his more ignominious activity as a slaver had been relegated to history's footnotes. We knew even more about the Meermin— South Africa's own Amistad—from the extensive paper trail left in the wake of the trial of the survivors of the shipboard rebellion whose suppression ultimately led to that vessel's demise. La Cybele had wrecked in Table Bay in South Africa's Cape Town within sight of Table Mountain, and the rescue of the crew and the enslaved—all of whom survived—left an archival footprint. Even so, none of the accounts of these three events provided the "X-marks-the-spot" details that would readily lead us to the actual wreck sites.

Finding a specific shipwreck is never easy, but not always for the reasons one may think. Sometimes the question is not "Where do we look for the shipwreck?," but more a matter of "How do we sort out which of the shipwrecks we've located is the one we think it is?" Coastlines such as those where these three well-documented disasters occurred are often referred to in the lingo of archaeologists as "shiptraps": points where shifting winds whip up without warning, or a single inopportune reef is easily missed by an inattentive sailor or a captain navigating in unfamiliar waters. Claiming victim after victim over the centuries, these hazards often conspire to litter a few miles of shoreline with the remains of literally dozens of ill-fated vessels. In spite of our best efforts (still ongoing) to locate the Meermin, Le Jardinière, and La Cybele, to this very day they remain hidden in the archaeological record—despite their visibility in the historical one.

In stark contrast to all it had to say about those three ships, history provided but a glancing mention of the São José and its fate. At the outset, all we knew about the ship was gleaned from a reference another researcher made when, decades ago, he recorded a footnote that caught his eye as he combed through the dusty daily journals of the Dutch East India Company. A brief entry in the journal for December 1794 summarized the terrible story of the São José in a terse note that recorded "a Portuguese ship ran aground in a place called Camps Bay (approximately 6 kilometers from Cape Town) and 200 of the 500 slaves on board perished." Nowadays Camps Bay refers to an upscale community arrayed beneath the majestic peaks of the Twelve Apostles and spanning a mile-long stretch of beach, located no more than four miles from the heart of Cape Town. But in December 1794, it would have been a very different place.

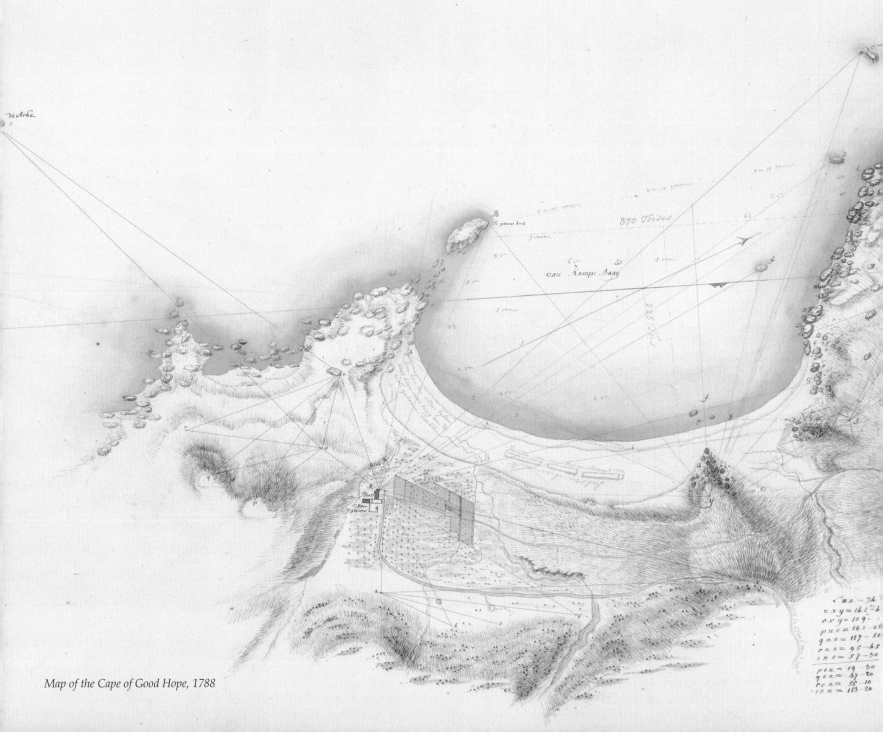

Map of the Cape of Good Hope, 1788

OCEAAN

Those few sobering handwritten lines indicated that the loss of liberty experienced on every slaving vessel had been compounded in this instance by a tragic loss of many lives. Most immediately for purposes of a search, it not only seemed to provide a very good idea about where the ship and those on board had met their fate, but it was also pointing to an area in which only one other shipwreck had ever been recorded—a relieving contrast to the locations in which we have searched for the more heavily documented slaver wrecks. Following in the track of the historians who had picked up on the original reference to the wrecking location and requoted it enough times to enshrine it as "undisputed fact," we therefore turned our attention to focus squarely on Camps Bay. As we would soon learn, facts of this "well known" sort may at times be misleading—perhaps all the more so by virtue of the veneer of authenticity afforded to them by scholarly repetition.

Kalk Baay

We also immediately recognized the potential importance of the information that this footnote provided about the São José's destination in the Americas, and its origin in Mozambique, on the east coast of Africa. By 1794, many millions of enslaved people had already sailed from West Africa across the Atlantic on many thousands of voyages and vessels. The slave trade from East Africa, however, was in its infancy. Just over a year before the São José weighed anchor, the Portuguese crown had revoked a longstanding prohibition against bringing enslaved people from its colony of Mozambique to Brazil. This reversal of policy was both a response to the rising demand for them in Brazil and a calculated effort by the monarchy to retain as much profit as possible by limiting this taxable trade to an exchange between its own colonies on the two sides of the Atlantic. The very first vessel to successfully complete this route is documented to have arrived in Rio de Janeiro in 1795. We now knew, however, it was not the first to make the attempt, since the São José had endeavored to sail the same route a year earlier. We realized that the shipwreck we were now intent on finding represented one of the very first efforts—and maybe even the pioneering one—to bring enslaved East Africans across the Atlantic.

East Africa's role in the Atlantic slave trade is largely forgotten by the public. This is not entirely surprising, since the handful of dramatic accounts that have familiarized the public with the slave trade (such as the Hollywood blockbuster *Amistad* or the famous television series "Roots") all start the story in West Africa. Most South Africans are thus quite surprised to hear that slavers bound for the Americas once plied their coasts, while Americans have sometimes set out to correct us when we begin to discuss the archaeological evidence of the trade from East Africa ("don't you mean West Africa?"). This orientation is mirrored by historical scholarship, which—as a whole—treats the East African trade as a sort of addendum to the main event.

In part, this is because the slave trade from East Africa for centuries sent the enslaved primarily in the opposite direction, to destinations around the rim of the Indian Ocean, and was drawn in earnest into the transatlantic orbit only during the last few decades of the trade to the Americas. When this happened, however, it did so with a vengeance, so that in the relatively short period between 1780 and 1870, nearly half a million East Africans joined the roughly ten to eleven million West Africans brought in chains across the Atlantic. What began as barely a trickle at the end of the eighteenth century would thus eventually surge into a torrent of enslaved humanity, feeding the increasingly voracious appetite of the plantation economies of Brazil as well as Cuba at the height of their growth throughout the first half of the nineteenth century. Thus, while fewer than a dozen slave ships arrived in Rio de Janeiro from Mozambique before 1811, more than eighty-five ships made the same voyage between 1825 and 1829, bearing a total of more than forty-eight thousand enslaved East Africans in their holds. The historian Herbert Klein informs us that by 1830, just under eleven thousand enslaved Africans were being sent across the Atlantic from that continent's east coast each and every year.

Surging demand for the enslaved was not the only factor that sent slavers scrambling for new sources on the other side of the African continent. Ironically, the growing success of those campaigning against the slave trade played a role in this shift as well. In 1807 abolitionists convinced the British government to pass the first laws against slave trading in its own colonies. Over the three decades that followed, this former slaving power cajoled other major nations implicated in the trade to pass a series of treaties that, by 1836, finally rendered it illegal everywhere to trade in human captives. East Africa initially grew into an important source of enslaved people as the earliest of these treaties rendered more established sources in West Africa illegal. Once the trade became illegal everywhere, slavers found they could continue to perpetrate the trade with greater impunity along the remote Indian Ocean coast of the continent, where the British anti-slavery squadrons were deployed in far fewer numbers than found along the more accessible West African coast.

The profits from these new East African sources were reaped at a horrific price—one that exacted an even greater toll in human suffering than was already characteristic of this inhumane enterprise. If the horrors of the Middle Passage typically culled the lives of so many in a voyage that on average took just over a month from West Africa across the Atlantic, they often demanded a much higher toll from the ghastly holds of those slave ships compelled to stay far longer—sixty days on average at sea, because they were coming from the other coast of the continent.

By the time East Africa had become a significant source for the transatlantic trade, the United States Congress had, in 1808, banned slave trading to U.S. ports and prohibited U.S. citizens from participating in slave trading. Nevertheless, American citizens, industries, and indeed the very American flag itself all became centrally important in the perpetration of the transatlantic slave trade for many decades after these laws

List of officers and crew of the São José Paquete d'Africa, *from Lisbon to Mozambique, under Captain Manuel João. Dated Moçambique, 31, July, 1794.*

Lista dos Officiaes, & Equipa

gem do Navio S. Joze Paquete d'Africa vindo
da Cidade d'Lisboa p.ª a Moçambique anno de

1794

Cap.ᵐ .... " Manoel João
Capelão .... " O R.ᵈᵒ Manoel Ignacio
1.º Piloto .... " Joze Ribeyro Augusto   } 6
2.ᵈᵒ .... " Joze Maria Vieira
3.º .... " Manoel Joze d'Oliveira
Serurgião ... " Antonio Vieira

                                                    " 10

Contram.ᵉ .... }
Carpinteiro .. }
Calafate ...... }   4
Tanoeiro ...... }

        Marinheiros, Mancebos, e Moços   25
                    Por todos   "   35

. Moçambique 31. de Julho de 1794 a f.ᵗ

            Manoel João

had been passed. In the process of researching the story of the São José, many indications of this American involvement have come to light in the archives—sometimes pointing in new and startling directions that deserve additional future research in their own right.

Thus we have learned that American captains and slave ships were familiar with these shores well before the trade was banned in the United States. Their names (Benjamin Moore, Thomas Beller, James William) appear in the logs of the harbor masters of Mozambique's slaving ports from Inhambane in the far south to Mozambique Island in the north. Just a few months before the São José weighed anchor under the command of the Portuguese captain Manuel João, two American vessels—one from Boston and the other from Rhode Island—arrived in Mozambique seeking slaves. Over the next few years other vessels from U.S. ports would follow, arriving from New York, Newport, Charleston, and Boston. It is more than likely that Beller and Moore—along with several other American captains who registered departures with cargoes of captives from Mozambique Island—would have crossed paths with the owner of the São José (who would remain active as a slaver until 1828) at the seat of the local municipal government on Mozambique Island, a building that stands to this day, and whose cornerstone inscription tells us had been erected merely a decade before the São José was lost.

The American flag became a particularly important tool in the perpetration and perpetuation of the slave trade as it slid treaty by treaty into illegality. Whereas the British eventually compelled nation after nation to sign treaties that allowed the British to board and search ships suspected of slaving, the

American flag remained exempt. This was thanks to a key provision that had ended the war of 1812 by addressing a longstanding American grievance against British interference with its ships on the high seas. It demonstrated how increasingly adept slavers had become at manipulating the fine points of international law in order to dodge legal restrictions. They often carried crews and captains of multiple nationalities and parallel sets of official papers, which would allow them to shift the flags under which they sailed as dictated by convenience or necessity. Thus the American flag was often hoisted on both coasts of Africa and both sides of the Atlantic, as a shield that safeguarded slavers and their trade.

Though the slave trade's final decades present a challenge because of the sparseness with which illegal activities are always documented, slaving voyages from Africa to the United States are well known to have happened as late as 1859. The very last documented slaving voyage across the Atlantic (to Cuba) occurred in 1867. If the slave trade often seems a distant and unfamiliar past, we are reminded of how recent it really was if we consider that, by the time of that final voyage, steamships were already crossing the Atlantic (and a handful were, in fact, slavers), while the two Wright brothers, future inventors of the airplane—a mode of transportation in whose holds we traverse the Atlantic in hours rather than months—had both already been born.

As we searched for the São José, we knew we were looking for perhaps the very first measure that had breathed additional decades of life into the slave trade, bringing it to the very threshold of our modern world, and adding hundreds of thousands of souls to the roster of those carried across the Atlantic into bondage.

RECOVERY 2011

For over two years, from 2011 to 2013, we searched Camps Bay for the submerged site of the São José in vain. In work season after season, Jaco, frequently assisted by Jonathan Sharfman and Tara Van Niekerk from SAHRA (the South African Heritages Resource Agency), led several Slave Wrecks Project teams in magnetometer searches of Camps Bay. (A magnetometer is a geophysical instrument that measures the earth's magnetic field and that will identify ferrous objects—including those characteristic of shipwrecks such as ships' fittings, iron guns, anchors, and nails—as an anomaly or variance in the normal magnetic field.) At different times Steve and students from The George Washington University joined in, as well as National Park Service colleagues volunteering their expertise during personal leave—all to no avail. Although in the course of these surveys we identified several magnetic anomalies, further inspection dives proved them to be bits of an old pipeline, a relatively modern anchor, and assorted types of discarded modern metallic refuse. Frustrated and confounded, we returned to the archives again—Jaco to the records of the Dutch East India Company in Cape Town, Steve to the Mozambican holdings in the Archives of Overseas History in Lisbon.

'TWO HUNDRED AND TWELVE SLAVES PERISHING'

Jaco made the most important breakthrough first. After many hours of rifling through the stuffy tomes of the Dutch East India Company, he happened across a deposition a Portuguese captain gave to a local Dutch lawyer about the shipwrecking of his vessel. It was none other than the São

José! Or, as we now learned its full name, the *São José Paquete d'Africa.* In his deposition, the captain testified that the ship had left Lisbon on 27 April 1794, destined for Mozambique, to take on board a cargo of enslaved Africans with the order to sail to Maranhão in Brazil. On her way from Mozambique with her cargo of captives, she was sailing toward Cape Town hoping to re-supply, but on the night of 27 December 1794, a strong southeasterly wind prevented the crew from entering safe anchorage at Table Bay. They decided, therefore, to hug the coast and hope that better conditions would allow them to enter Table Bay the following day — a decision that turned out to be a tragically fateful one. According to the deposition: "…at two o'clock in the morning, as they sought to re-secure anchors belatedly noticed as having been dragging throughout the night, the ship struck a rock and started taking water while, according to the Captain, under a well-known landmark: the Lion's Head."

The deposition continues in a lawyerly, efficient, almost bulletin-like bureaucratic prose that seems intent on conveying just the bare facts about the dramatic events that transpired throughout the remainder of the night and into the early dawn:

> …the captain ordered the crew to cast out an anchor, but the cable snapped. They dropped a second anchor and then realized that the stern of the vessel was stuck on rock. The strong wind and surge broke this anchor as well and the ship now became wedged between two reefs. The crew then tried to use the ship's windlass and a third anchor to get the ship off the rocks, but this rope broke as well. The captain and crew now realized that they were close to the shore and sent a boat with a line

ashore. In the rough seas this small boat was broken up in the process of coming ashore. Next, a raft with sailors and slaves aboard was sent ashore, along with another small boat. In the meantime, a Dutch East India Company official from Cape Town arrived and rigged a basket on a rope which they were able to attach to the ship and begin to bring the people and some of the slaves to safety.

"Unfortunately," the captain concludes matter-of-factly, "the sea became so rough that the ship broke up and became a total wreck with two hundred and twelve slaves perishing in the violent waves."

The reference to the shipwreck occurring "under a well-known landmark" immediately refocused our sights with respect to the physical search for the shipwreck site. Rather than Camps Bay, the description in the wrecking account seemed to point instead toward Clifton, a smaller cove just to the north, its landscape clearly dominated by this looming and iconic promontory still known today as the Lion's Head.

In fact, Jaco already knew of a shipwreck there, long referred to by the local dive community as the "Schuylenburg site." Supposedly this was the final resting place of a Dutch East India Company supply vessel that had disappeared without a trace during a journey between Cape Town and nearby Simon's Town in 1756. Further investigation revealed that the amateur treasure hunter who had first discovered the wreck site in the 1980s had been seeking a name that would allow him to meet permitting requirements, which required that a site be given the designation of a known maritime loss. He selected "Schuylenburg" primarily because it fit the bill—being both a wreck that had never been found elsewhere, and that had disappeared while undertaking

Letter dated 27 January 1795, written in Portuguese, documenting and contesting the sale of a captive African aboard the São José. Excerpt:

"...having been Informed that Joaquim de Aranha e Oliveira intended to sell the negro he had stationed on the Sheikh of Mongincual's galleys in order to repay his debt, and believing he would not fail to fulfill his promise, I refrained from pressing this summons...until it came to my attention that he had sold that slave to the ship of Captain Manuel João, departed from this port on the third day of this month, and having since requested repayment of the debt owed, continued to be misled by him without receiving any satisfaction...the issuing of an embargo upon his goods is now requested of the Judge of the Royal Treasury in the amount required to repay this unpaid debt...."

Informação que Sobre Me deu o Ajudante da
das minhas Ordens, e Despacho, q. proferi com
Data de 8 de Novembro do Prezente anno no
Requerim.to da inclusa Sup.te lhe diféra como julgar ser
de Direito. Palacio de S. Paulo 22 de Dezem-
bro de 1794// E ambos os d.os Despachos foraõ
Rubricados pelo Gov.or /

Está conforme o Off.al Maio Mathias Piis Vianna

a voyage that would have brought it past Clifton. Despite being a product of administrative convenience rather than of any substantive investigation of the site itself, the name had stuck. Over time it had gained the status of "fact"—one that had not caught our interest until the captain's deposition forced us to scrutinize it in a whole new way.

If we did not yet know that the wreck was that of the São José, it became apparent almost as soon as we started diving that it could not be the Schuylenburg. The first hints that the site had been misidentified came in the form of the copper sheathing, nails, and spikes we found. We knew that shipbuilders had started to use copper fastenings and sheathing to protect the bottoms of wooden ships plying tropical waters from shipworms only later in the eighteenth century—well after the Schuylenburg had disappeared. The four cannons on the site also seemed to rule out the only other possible candidate in the historical record—the Hopefield Packet, a small, thirty-one-ton coastal schooner that ran aground in Camps Bay in 1869, after the crew and captain got drunk while sailing her to Dyer Island with general stores. Not only would a coastal schooner have been unlikely to carry any guns, but further review of the archival account shows that following the grounding, the hull had been sold for £75, suggesting it had likely been re-floated. Moreover, the cargo had been sold for a mere £125.

'1130 IRON BARS'

Over the next two years, as we struggled through unseasonable storms that severely reduced what were already the slimmest of work windows the weather would permit, evidence began to

mount that this might well be the site of the São José. According to the captain's deposition, the ship had become "wedged between two rocks," and at a distance that was close enough to the shore to allow a rescue line to be rigged that was capable of carrying survivors in a basket from the distressed vessel to the beach. The signs of wreckage and the artifacts we were finding were located between and upon two reefs, and within the limited distance from shore that would allow such a line to be tied. Even the captain's accounts of the depth at which the ship ran aground proved to be consistent with what we were finding.

Meanwhile, a review of the treasure hunter's report on the limited work he had done on site before he had lost interest was also suggestive. It included ceramics identifications that, ironically, ruled out his own designation of the site as that of the Schuylenburg. They were, however, consistent with the alternative possibility of the São José. More speculatively, he also mentioned a large number of "horseshoe"-shaped objects cemented to portions of the reef (but which had since deteriorated and were no longer visible on site). Knowing that shackles often were U-shaped like horseshoes, we wondered….

Our suspicion that this was the wreck of the São José gained even more validation as new archaeological findings on the site in South Africa and new documentary evidence brought to light in Portugal pointed directly at each other. Working with his team in the field, Jaco had uncovered another important artifact on the site: solid iron blocks, each about two feet in length, which were easily recognizable as a kind of iron ballast that had been used to stabilize sailing ships.

Starting in the late eighteenth century, iron ballast is known to have been used by slave ship captains who were concerned that human bodies did not weigh enough, nor were they packed as compactly as other types of cargo (despite being shackled back-to-back and crammed in rows on decks so low it was not possible to stand) to ensure a center of gravity low enough to safeguard their vessel's stability. Iron ballast could compensate for human bodies in other, more literal ways as well, at times serving as a good traded for enslaved people— one commodity traded for another.

The ballast that we found became more than a suggestion that this might be the site of a slave ship, and the particular one we were looking for, when Steve and long-time archival research collaborator Yolanda Teixeira Duarte excitedly pored over the most recent find. Clearly noted in the very first line of the ledger of the São José's cargo manifest when it had left Lisbon at the outset of its voyage was this entry: "1130 iron bars."

GHOSTLY ECHOES

How is it, then, that shipwreck sites come to be identified? Archaeologists rarely find a ship's bell with the name of the ship engraved, nor do most vessels exhibit unique or iconic features such as those that make some famous ships such as the Titanic or the Monitor so readily recognizable. In fact, most shipwrecks don't look much like anything more than a pile of stones, or a strangely straight edge embedded in a reef, something the untrained eye can easily miss when swimming over it. Once they are found, many are at best remnants of vessels that, after being catastrophically dismembered in the first place, may well have suffered the additional ravages of repeated storms or salvage. They will have disappeared and reappeared over

Mappa da Carga que conduis o Navio denominado S. Jozé Paquete de Africa
do Porto da Cidade de Lisboa para o de Moçambique do qual é Capitão Manoel João em o Anno de

1794

Ferro em Barras	Barris de Polvora	Barris d'Vinho	Barris de Molhado	Barris de Seco	Bahus
1:130	122	81	31	46	6
Frasqr.ª d'Agoa ardte. Alz	Cx.ª d'V engarrafado	Caixas de Seco	Sacas de Seco	Ancor.tas de Azei. & Figos	Caixão de Botica
60	5	10	7	18	1
Caixas de Coral	Barr. d'Missg. & Inclorio	Barris & Bordens d'Milho	Barrilr.ª d'Passas & Alz.ᵗᵃ	Canastras d'Melroa	Salas de Queijos
1	21	25	32	6	4
Fardos	Caixotes	Pipas de Azeite	Fateixas	Mezas	Embrulhos
1	9	1	13	7	1

Manoel João

Cargo manifest for the São José Paquete d'Africa, from Lisbon to Mozambique,
1794. Top row (l-r): iron bars, 1130; gunpowder, 122 barrels; wine, 81 barrels;
liquids, 31 barrels; dry goods, 46 barrels.

time, covered and re-covered in the sand brought by currents or storms, or submerged under the gradual growth of reefs. Archaeology on such sites is like trying to piece together a puzzle in which half the pieces have gone missing, while some of those that remain have been thrown into a blender.

More often than not, the case for identifying a ship will necessarily have to be circumstantial—yet in order to do so, the case must always be substantial. Confidence rises as independent lines of evidence emerge, each failing to contradict the hypothesis and instead continuing—time after time—to corroborate each other. This has proved to be the case of the shipwreck we are now quite certain is the São José— the site described so specifically with reference to landmarks and to a configuration of reefs that trapped and doomed it, doing so at particular depths and at prescribed distances from shore, and in an area well monitored in its day. Even today, the site continues to surrender artifact after artifact that insist on pointing to the same timeframe and telling the same tale that documents in disparate archives tell—from the late eighteenth-century pulley block to the concretions whose X-rays reveal the ghostly echo of what once was a shackle.

Several large timbers that Jonathan Sharfman, one of the divers on the research team, found at the end of a working dive have provided the most recent corroborating evidence. Hoping for more information, we took samples and sent them to Dr. Marion Bamford, a world-renowned timber specialist at the University of the Witwatersrand, Johannesburg. Her laboratory analysis identified the timbers as *Dalbergia melanoxylon*, an extremely rare hardwood still to be found on the mainland about sixty kilometers from the Island of Mozambique where the enslaved from the São José embarked. Perhaps these timbers were carried as dunnage, on top of the iron ballast. Meanwhile, one of the structural timbers we have located on site has been identified as another type of East African mangrove wood, perhaps part of a repair—a suggestion that has emerged from yet additional archival evidence that ships were frequently repaired on the island, a fact long forgotten by official histories. Further analysis will tell us more, as will the excavation work that proceeds on the site. As we continue to unravel the mysteries on this archaeological site, the cumulative convergence of so many independent lines of corroborating evidence establish beyond any reasonable doubt that we are working on the remains of the slaver, *São José Paquete d'Africa*.

Scan and image of concretized shackle

Timber from hull

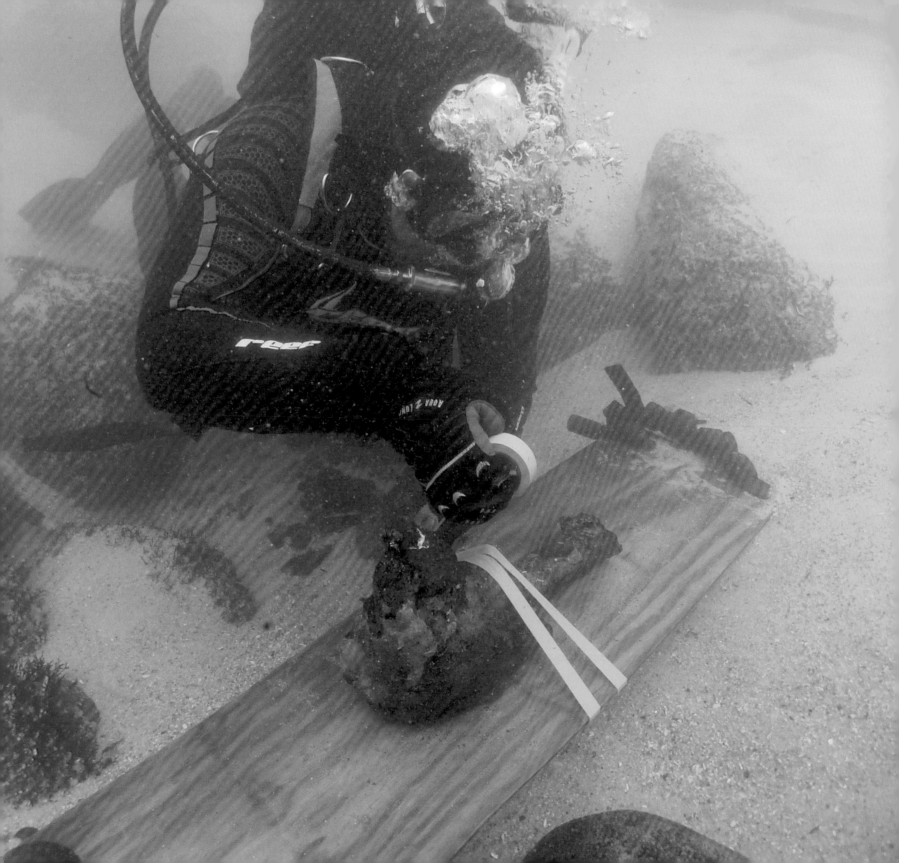

VOYAGE December 27, 1794

Only part of what we know about this voyage and the final moments of those on board has been gleaned from the archives and artifacts. It is the site itself that has often insisted on inscribing its most visceral insights through the rigors and risks it imposes on each of us in the research team, as we attempt to work on it under water. It is a site that is almost always difficult—and more often than not, simply too dangerous—to dive. Exposed to the prevailing southeasterly winds, a back reef creates a swell break whose surge is amplified by the site's relative shallowness and proximity to the beach. Even in moderate weather, skilled divers find themselves swinging back and forth in a sweeping and erratic pendulum motion. The effort and focus required to combat the surge in order to excavate or document can easily distract even the most experienced diver…just long enough for the drift to allow the next surge to dash him or her against the reef. We have all bled on this site.

The constant swirl of sand reduces visibility and has at one time or another disoriented every single diver who has worked with us, forcing each one to the surface in an effort to find lost bearings. Archaeological documentation is made all the more challenging when an area uncovered on a first laborious dive is found upon return, a mere hour or two later, to have already been re-covered by a foot or more of sand. Years of contending with these challenges have impressed upon us that our dive tanks and computers, our fins and our masks, render us at best only marginally less helpless than those who found themselves on the distressed and disintegrating São José on that December eve so long ago.

ENTOMBED

The suffering of those on board the São José had begun even before they reached Mozambique Island to embark on its fatal voyage. Then—as is also the case today—one could arrive at this slaving outpost by land or by sea. Some of the enslaved would have endured the long trek by foot, taking weeks to traverse the distances between Nampula in the interior and Mozambique Island that our Jeeps now cover in mere hours. They would have taken their final steps on African soil staggering along the same paths still used today across the marsh flats of Mossuril or of Quintagona. The vista of the bay surrounding Mozambique Island would have filled most— who had never seen the sea—with both amazement and fear. Likely kept first for days or even weeks in the slave pens of the slave traders' compounds, whose ruins are still evident across this landscape, they would have eventually been herded into small dhows and shuttled under careful guard to the slave ships awaiting in the anchorage on the north side of the island. To those seeing them for the first time and bound for their holds, these ships would have loomed as giant and terrible apparitions holding the promise of unknown horrors.

Others, arriving by a different route from the sea, would have already experienced those horrors, having been brought down the Zambezi River and then north along the coast from Quelimane by boat, before being disembarked and hurried into the temporary holding pens of one of the many slave traders found on the island itself. In both cases—and as had already happened several times along their route, when the enslaved were first purchased far inland, and again when passing through the lands of the surrounding sheikhs—the traders on the mainland or the island would have exacted their pound of flesh from the captain of the São José in exchange for the exhausted and shrinking human frames. At least one document tells us in detail of the wranglings involved in the sale of an enslaved African to the captain of the São José just days before that vessel's departure. (See pages 40 and 41.)

Those on board the São José had already been at sea for three weeks on the night they heard the sound of splintering timbers and felt the icy grip of water pouring in as the reefs of Clifton set out to dismember their floating prison. Packed together in the ship's hold, these five hundred bodies would already have endured weeks of the sweltering heat at the very height of summer in the Southern Hemisphere. It was a voyage timed to beat the Indian Ocean monsoons and catch the tail end of the Atlantic's favorable trade winds, but utterly indifferent to human suffering. Spent by this ordeal, it is more than likely some were sick and dying, many were seasick and dehydrated, and all were weak and worn. Every captive on board was in some stage of physical distress long before the ship ever was.

What the captain's curt account fails to reveal about the drama that unfolded throughout the final hours of the São José we can still imagine with some certainty. Struggling to breathe in the heat of a hold, swamped with the stifling stench of sweat and urine, the enslaved would have found themselves awash in their own vomit, or that of the other enslaved succumbing in droves to the nauseating unrest of the violent sea. Entombed in the lightless hold of a ship shrouded by the pitch black of a storm-tossed night, surely the next of the human senses to be overwhelmed would have been that of sound. As awareness of the ship's plight took hold amongst the crew — and as sheer panic

55

heeuwierpen en als toen bevonden dat het touw van het eerste anker
was gebrooken; dat het Schip voor het tweede anker optorneende,
Zij Comparanten bevonden, dat het agter Schip op een klip Stootede,
het welk met zodanig een geweld aankwam dat door alle de
haaken en vingerlingen braaken, en also het roer afstootede, Schoon
het zelve nog aan de Zorg lijnen bleef hangen; dat vermits de donkerheid
der nagt, welke al zeer Sterk was, Zij Comparanten, in de grootste
bekommernis, het aankoomen van den dag afwagten, en het loot wierpen
en bevonden op neegen vadem water en tusschen twee Klippen te
leggen, wanneer zij aanstonds de boot en Schuijt uitzetten, om het
Schip daartusschen uitteboegseeren; dat het gevaar van tijd tot tijd
toeneemende Zij Comparanten een werp anker en twee nieuwe
Touwen uitbrengen, om met het Spil, waar aan al het Scheepsvolk
was, het Schip nog buiten de boegseering, uittewinden, dan dat door de
Sterke branding en de hol lopende Zee, het Schip zodanig zwaar
werkte dat de touwen braaken, waarop des Equipants en Zij Comparanten,
resolveerden, om de fok, kluijver, groot en klijn marszeil bijtemaaken
om te zien het nog van Strand te houden; dan dat de wind geduurig
varieerende en Zijcomparanten geen gebruik van het zoor hebbende
hun derde anker presenteerden, dan waar na het Schip op een
allergeweldigste wijze op de grond en klippen Stootede, waardoor het
zelve geheel lek wierd en daarom beslooten het Cargasoen, Slaaven, en
het volk te redden, vermits de behouding van het Schip onmogelijk
was; dat zij daarop een Schuijt met Slaaven naar de wal zonden,
welke ook behouden arriveerden, Dog door de zwaare branding

niet konde te rug koomen, terwijl gelijkentijd de Chaloup teegens
Strand aan Stukken sloeg; dat zij gedaa Comparanten also hun
Chaloup en Schuit missende en het gevaar hand over hand aanneemende
om zij neevens de Slaaven te redden, een vlot maakten, en het zelve met
eenige manschap en Slaaven naar de wal zonden, zonder dat er eenige
mogelijkheid was dat het zelve vlot weeder te rug konde koomen, terwijl
inmiddels de zond houte, om het Schip spoelde, waardoor men belet
wierd de kleijne Schuit aan boord te krijgen en waarop de boots man over
boord sprong om zij te redden en met de kleijne Schuit aan de wal is
gekoomen; dat zij Comparanten in de hoop van hulp van deeze plaats
te zullen bekoomen, tragten een touw aan de wal te krijgen, wanneer eenen
neeger uuren de masten de een na den anderen neevens het wandt over
boord sloegen; dat zij Adsistentie van het Gouvernement hebbende
bekoomen en een heen en weeder door een touw en mande hebbende
gemaakt, also hebben gecontinueerd om daardoor eenige van de manschappen
en Slaaven te sauveeren tot des avonds ten vijf uuren, wanneer het
Schip aan Stukken sloeg, waardoor zij naderhand bevonden, dat twee hon-
derd Twaalf Slaaven, welke zij hadden zoeken te redden, verongelukt waaren, terwijl
de overige welke zij neevens de verongelukte nog ten tijde van het
Stukken slaan van het Schip, op het zelve hadden bevonden, gelukkig
aande wal zij gekoomen. – Dat zij Comparanten voorts bij het wrak
van het Schip zij gebleeven en Zorgvuldig voor al wat aan de wal
spoelde hebben gezorgd en opgepast tot den [...] deezer [...]
naderhand een publijque verkooping te doen houden

Depositions by São José captain Manuel João and crew dated 29, December 1794, recorded in Dutch, on the wrecking of the São José off Cape Town. Excerpt:

"The company arrived at this remote place when the wind rose in such a way from the southeast that is was impossible to enter here, into Table Bay, like it is normal in this case….

The company, in the greatest anxiety, waited for the arrival of the day, threw the anchor, and found themselves run aground on two rocks….

They therefore sent a boat of slaves to the shore, which arrived safely, but because of a dangerous surf it could not return….

The ship broke to pieces, through which they afterwards found out that 212 slaves which tried to save themselves died."

set in after it struck the reef—the enslaved would have heard desperately shouted orders, punctuated by sailors swearing in one breath, before perhaps invoking their patron saint in the very next. Hurled in Portuguese over groaning timbers and the cracking whip of sails, these invocations would have mingled with prayers to Allah or pleas for protection to the ancestors uttered in a variety of tongues—Macua, Sena, Yao, Makonde.

SALVAGE

As the ultimate fate of the vessel became clear, the captain and other officers with a financial interest in the venture would have ordered the crew to bring the weakened and terrified captives on deck—perhaps in small groups, to better control them. The officers would have done so in order to salvage as much of their investment as possible. As the night progressed, only a rump crew would have been left behind to ferry the enslaved across on the lifeline and basket that had eventually been rigged to the disintegrating ship, and through which most of the crew had already reached safety. At some point, however, those of the crew left behind must have read some sign of the vessel's imminent demise—perhaps an ominous shuddering of the deck or structural timbers finally shattering under the weight of the hammering waves. Whatever it was, at some point all the crew abandoned the ship together, leaving perhaps as many as half of the enslaved still on board—something we know because the record tells us all the crew survived, whereas more than two hundred of the enslaved did not.

As the ship finally broke apart, the early morning air would

Copper sheathing

have resounded with the shrieks of those injured or drowning — played out against the deafening drumbeat of the relentlessly crashing waves and the concluding, calamitous crescendo of the ship breaking apart. The final clamors of the doomed may well have been brief, as the angry sea would have claimed its victims quickly. Any still in the hold would have been instantly entombed. Others weighted by shackles or chained to each other would have been dragged beneath the surface in mere moments. Indeed, it is highly unlikely that many of those still on board ever made it to shore once the ship finally broke apart — even though it was a mere few hundred feet away. Most of the enslaved would have been weakened, and few, if any, would have known how to swim. Most of those not overcome by the towering waves, or battered by the swirl of jagged debris, would have quickly succumbed to the frigid waters that are ushered into this cove by Antarctic currents (a shock to many of the divers working with us on the site who had presumed the water must be warm because this was Africa). A few may have struggled in vain to break free of the entangled netting in which slave ships could sometimes be found ensconced — drawn down by the very web that the crew spun in their effort to protect their profits by thwarting suicide attempts, a final act of despair that became all too common during the course of the crossing.

Within just a few hours, the dozens of broken bodies carried to the beach by the churning surf would have coalesced into a ragged line stretched along the cove. At first toyed with by the surf, they would have grown increasingly motionless as the water released them from its grip and left them behind at the high-tide mark, entangled in the jumbled debris of the broken ship. The site of crew and locals disentangling those bodies from other cargo, only to cast them aside as refuse in order to salvage what was still of any value, is quite likely one of the last images seared into the memory of the survivors as they were herded away by other crew members and the Dutch officials who had come to the crew's aid.

The archival record tells us that all these traumatized survivors were auctioned off to local owners in the Cape—save eleven, we are told, who perished in the days following the wreck, perhaps too spent or injured by that ordeal to survive any other.

JOURNEY 1794-2015 (AND BEYOND)

It has sometimes been said that the past is a different country—and as researchers, we seek out all the evidence we can find to get there. In part, what we strive to do is to translate the behaviors and mind-sets that we find there and that seem so different—even alien—into terms that are in some sense comprehensible here in the present. That proves easier to do when we encounter at least something in the mix of the behaviors described in the document or suggested by the artifact that we can, at least in some way, relate to ourselves.

As archaeologists who work on and under the water, there are thus at least some aspects of the thinking on that vessel that we can readily grasp, even if more than two centuries separate us. The sea still demands that we account for the weight of our own bodies when we calculate boat-carrying capacity, imposing a metric that is indifferent to whether this weight is attributed to human or other forms of cargo—equipment, fuel—that we carry on board. In this sense, there is something in the captain's calculation of both iron bars and bodies as ballast that we can readily grasp.

But our efforts at translation are partial at best, since we inevitably encounter chasms that can prove much harder to span. It thus requires a far greater effort to grasp the column in that captain's ledger in which those iron bars and human beings were converted into the forms of shared monetary value that allowed them to be exchanged for each other in the marketplace.

The outward silence and stillness of the archives can be deceptive, inasmuch as the voices of the past arrested therein can still pack a blindsiding punch. The sheer matter-of-factness with which a slaver captain's account distinguishes "the people" from "the slaves" can subject you to a form of cognitive whiplash, as the oddity of this phrasing first forces a double-take, and then a dawning realization of its mundane presumption of difference in the very humanity of the enslaved and the crew. No less shocking—and revealing—are the precisely hand-drawn graphs by petty government officials of the day. Intent on conveying different measures of trade and commerce relevant to their administrative tasks and duties, they carefully tallied the enslaved with other commodities and trade goods, neatly listing them in tidy columns alongside goats, barrels of pitch, dry fish, bolts of cloth—the crass calculus through which Africans were shorn of their humanity and reduced to monetary value.

The handcrafted Excel spreadsheets of their day, these precisely rendered pie

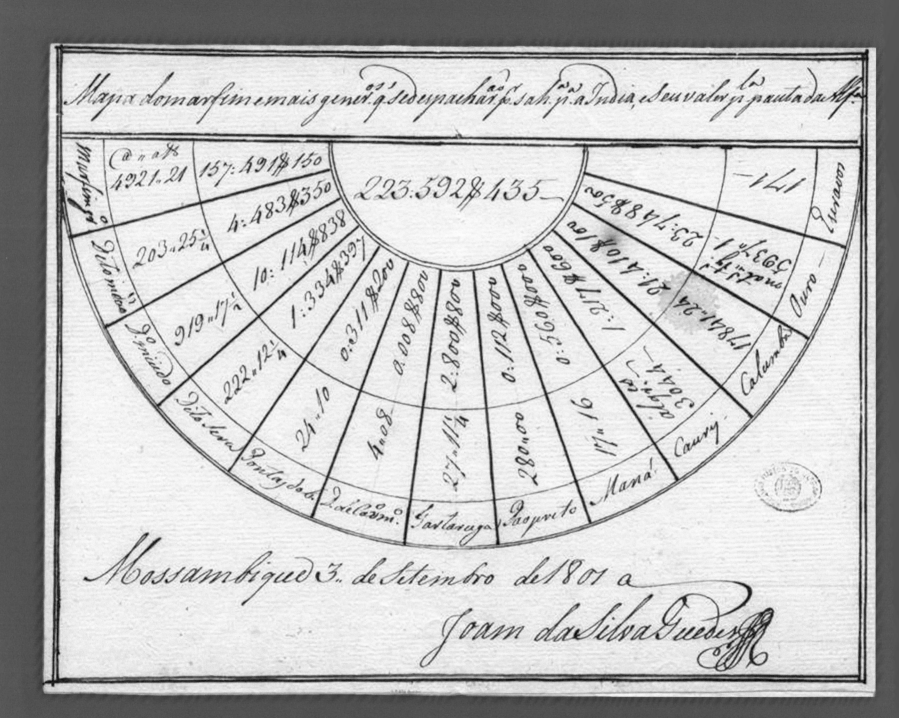

Table dated 3 September 1801, Mossambique, of ivory and other commodities cleared for export to India, and their value as determined by Customs: Large ivory tusks…Hippopotamus teeth…Tortoises…Ebony wood…Cowry shells…Gold…Slaves.

charts and ingeniously designed graphs force us to contemplate a past that is not only a different country, but a far more distant one. Perhaps it is for the very reason that they seem so alien, and because they are so profoundly unsettling, that these seemingly more distant pasts can more easily be—and often are—forgotten. We would contend that the responsibility of research in such instances is redoubled—to not merely translate, but to seek out and recover the inconvenient truths of the past that have been sanitized from history and bleached into invisibility.

FAITH AND CRUELTY

It is through this task of recovery that research comes to disturb—and so, ultimately, serve—the present. Certainly such acts of recovery disturb the settled, accepted, and dominant narratives about the past by bringing to light portions of this history that have been relegated to neglect or selective remembrance, or that have even sometimes been suppressed outright. Research can recast our understanding of what actually happened, re-introducing us to a journey we mistakenly think we know well. Our ongoing work on the São José has been punctuated with many instances of such eye-opening disturbances: that of a gold pendant found within yards of a shackle, underscoring the fact that luxurious privilege and suffering were both evident on these vessels. Or the names of individual enslaved Africans and the record of key life events such as marriage and baptism—found, against all expectations,

Barrel staves

in the archival records in Maranhão in Brazil—for more than one hundred Mozambicans who were transported on three other vessels that followed the São José's very same intended route with less fatally calamitous results.

In combing through archival accounts, we have been struck by how neglected the enslaved's resistance may be in our understanding of the slave trade, as we find that so many of the shipwrecks that have been added to the list of searches under way in the Slave Wrecks Project actually sank because of rebellions on board. We are continuously shocked by the enormous evidence of the ease with which fervent faith and the cruelty of the trade in flesh could co-habit—inasmuch as many hundreds of slaving vessels are documented as being named after dozens of different Christian saints, with no less than forty-seven of these invoking the same patron saint as that of the ship that ended so many lives in Clifton: Saint Joseph.

Recovery of such pasts—forgotten in the process of writing history—is part of the answer we give to those questions that are often posed to us: "Why do you do this work? Why seek out the shipwrecks of slavers? Why the Slave Wrecks Project?" Yet that is only part of the answer. If one measure of research is its capacity to disturb history through recovery of the past, another is its ability to utilize that capacity to disturb how we think of the future, by highlighting the connections between the conditions of the present and the past from which it springs. And thus, what is disturbing is not only what happened within the waves so long ago, nor even that this has since been forgotten, but rather, how what transpired over two centuries ago in this place is linked to what transpires there today.

The slave trade represented by this wreck is one link in a long chain of past conditions, each of which has meticulously shaped the link that followed, to cumulatively produce our shared present. Nowhere are these more prominently displayed than in the stark contrasts between the wealthy enclave of Clifton and the post-apartheid nation it is part of—a scenario that is played out again and again, in ways different but fundamentally the same, halfway around the world in the Americas.

Though the historical record recounts in some detail the disposition of all that was salvaged from the wreckage of the São José still deemed of any value, it remains markedly silent about where the bodies of the enslaved who died that day were buried. We suspect that the final resting place of those who perished would have been selected for its immediate convenience, and thus that the dead today lie under one or more of the luxury residences that crowd every valuable inch of real estate right up to the beach in this privileged community. What we can say with certainty is that, in being summoned from a forgotten past to represent the slave trade and its long legacy to the world, their final resting place provides a metaphor for illustrating how forgotten pasts undergird the present.

LOST LINKS, RECOVERED

If our research journey started with a search for the site of a shipwreck, it has brought us over time to the realization that the site of that story is far more extensive than we initially could have ever guessed. The journey of the São José extends in the most immediate sense from the interior of Mozambique, where enslavement first occurred, to a submerged site and the unknown graves somewhere near it, in a small cove in South Africa. It includes the descendants of its sold survivors, some of whom surely walk the streets of Cape Town today. It also encompasses the global enterprise of its owners, who mixed slaving with other business in locations as wide-ranging as India, Lisbon, Brazil, São Tomé, and Montevideo—a far-flung incidence of globalization two centuries before the term ever came into vogue.

It intersects with other stories whose protagonists walked streets—as slave traders or enslaved—in dozens of ports, and on hundreds of plantations scattered across the Western Hemisphere. Ultimately, the story of the São José is entangled with so many similar stories that insist we should strive to not forget about a brutal practice—the slave trade—that in all of its difficult detail laid the very cornerstone of modernity. Time after time as we have dived on the site of the São José, we have been reminded of the larger story that this archaeological remnant of merely one instance of the Middle Passage represents.

Understood in this light, the question of "Why the Slave Wrecks Project?" becomes moot. How can we not search for the evidence of what was so foundational in the formation of our modern world? How is it possible that such meager attention has been paid to studying and preserving the remnants of such a significant, and central, part of our past? How can we not reach out to recover these lost stories? What do we risk missing, as we build our future, if we do not examine its links with these pasts—if we do not fully understand the role of the Middle Passage in bringing us to where we now all are?

As maritime archaeologists, we know well that each time we dive beneath the waves, we hold the distinct privilege and sacred honor of searching for, and touching, what is perhaps the most literal embodiment of the Middle Passage.

And when we do, it always touches us back.

Approximate number of days the

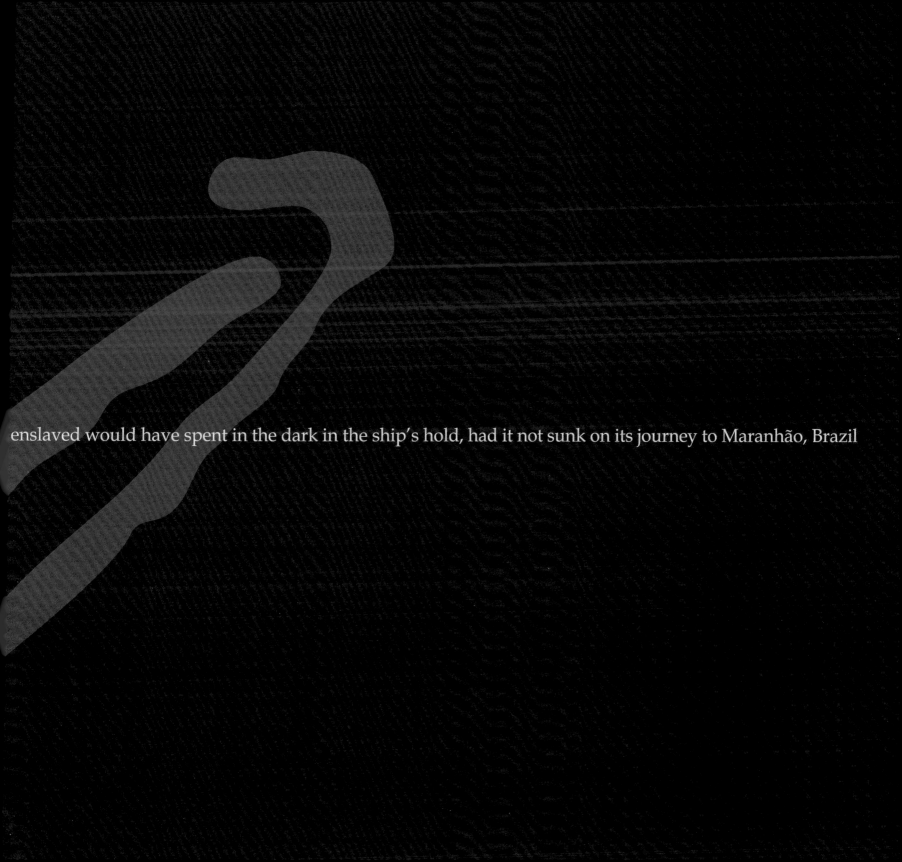

enslaved would have spent in the dark in the ship's hold, had it not sunk on its journey to Maranhão, Brazil

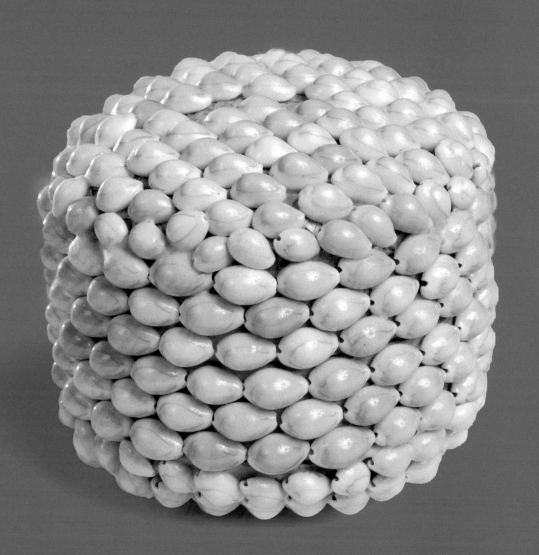

MOZAMBIQUE ISLAND
EAST AFRICA, May 29, 2015

It had been a journey.

Paul, Steve, and I had traveled from Washington, D.C., to Mozambique Island with other members of the Museum. We had come from a place that once too willingly welcomed enslaved Africans to a place where they had once been as efficiently exported as gunpowder, or beads, or any other commodity. We had flown over or near portions of the same Middle Passage that the enslaved who drowned off the South Africa coast would have endured in the cargo hold of the São José had the ship not capsized.

It was their journey, of course, that had brought us here. Our goal was to follow the route of the São José from Mozambique to South Africa, to grasp a sense of its meaning historically and metaphorically.

And to ensure that those souls once lost were now remembered.

WITNESS

I had not expected it to take as long as it had to be able to honor these ancestors of all African Americans. Finding the remains of a slaver that had wrecked with its human cargo on board (no need to say "ship carrying slaves" or even "slave ship," as these vessels were so common at one time) was a journey we began in 2005, when I became the director of the Smithsonian's newly conceived National Museum of African American History and Culture. Now, a decade later, and thanks to the extraordinary efforts of a consortium of institutions, we were commemorating the lives lost on just such a ship.

Part of the power of finding this ship was the immediacy and intimacy it brought to the almost unfathomable breadth of the story it was complicit in: the capturing and selling into bondage of approximately twelve million African men, women, and children. The enormity of the global slave trade can be difficult to comprehend. The unwitting testimony that the wreck of the São José leaves allows us to personalize the statistics: to humanize the souls of those enslaved, and to make their lives visible to the millions who will bear witness to the objects recovered from the ship.

HERITAGE

Mozambique Island was the capital of Portuguese East Africa during colonial rule. UNESCO has since named it a World Heritage Site. The architecture on certain parts of the island is amazing—classical European structures whose beauty was built with money from the slave trade. But vestiges of the long-

fought Mozambican Civil War in the late twentieth century still linger, and the struggling economy has resulted in these once-grand facades becoming faded — much like the memory of the area's once-thriving slave trade.

We had come to revive those memories and that history. It was clear to us, by the gracious reception we received from Mozambican officials as well as the American ambassador, that honoring those from this region whose lives were so profoundly altered by slavery was important to the people here.

It was also complicated.

Among those we were introduced to was a sheikh, Hafiz Jamu, whose family members had prospered because they had helped to sell their people into slavery. I could not imagine the pain and burden of carrying that history.

In the Memorial Garden to the Slave Trade, we scattered white roses into the sea, in memory of those on the São José who had drowned. The local tribespeople performed a series of dances as part of the ceremony. Some of the tribal chiefs attending were dressed in Portuguese military uniforms. *How should I react*, I wondered. It took me awhile to put the uniforms away in my head.

RAMP

We then made our way north into the island's interior to Mossuril, where we met with the Makua people, whose forebears had once revolted against the Portuguese. They told us that the dance we had seen, with some of the chiefs wearing those uniforms, were ones that had been performed to please the Portuguese slave traders. I was struck once more by how complicated this journey was.

The series of dances the Makua performed for us had very different rhythms from the earlier ones—an unmediated experience not intended for those who had come to capture and enslave. The Makua executed their performance on the site whose dusty ground had been ground zero for being sold into slavery. You could feel the presence of the enslaved everywhere, from the auction site to the homes of those without wealth.

I had been to numerous sites where enslaved Africans were housed and sold. Time and again—in Ghana, in Senegal, in Angola—I have been moved by the large forts and castles with gates and doorways of no return, through which captives would pass as they were loaded into the slave ships.

But here in Mozambique, it was different. There was no door or gate in Mossuril. Instead, there was something I had never before encountered, something perhaps more efficient for hastening captives onto their grim vessel: a Ramp of No Return.

I stepped onto the ramp and looked ahead of me, to a vista of sparkling water and attractive islands. This same beauty would have shown itself to the hundreds who had hobbled down the ramp in shackles, a beauty that belied the horror that lay just beyond.

I walked down the Ramp of No Return five times with various officials. But I knew that this was a journey of thirty yards that I also had to make alone, to honor those who never came home. The ramp was graded at an awkward angle, making it difficult to walk—and this was without shackles. Like so many who had gone before me, I looked at what was ahead of me, and realized that I could not see anything behind me. For the captives, it would have been as if all they had known simply vanished.

As I made my way to the end of the ramp one final time, this history that we had come here to commemorate was no longer distant, but immediate. And as an African American, extraordinarily real.

RAMPA DE ESCRAVOS
Protegida pela lei nº10/88, de 22 de /12
Determina a Protecção dos bens mate
riais e imateriais do Património cultural
Moçambicano-Ministério da cultura
Patrocinado pela:D.P.tur.

VESSEL

We had come to Mozambique, among other reasons, to take something away: some of the soil of the country, to scatter at the site of the wreck off South Africa's coast.

I had not given much thought as to what the receptacle for this soil should be. My focus had been on what we planned to do with it. But the highest-ranking chief of those we were now meeting with, Evano Nhogache, had given it much consideration. The soil would travel to South Africa in a beautiful cowrie shell vessel. When this wise man placed the basket in my hands, he told me that, in essence, bringing this soil to South Africa was no longer our notion; now, it was our ancestors' idea.

I felt a chill run through me as I held the vessel. It was as if I were holding the spirits of our ancestors. I could feel a spiritual weight upon me, and for a few moments, I was simply taken away, thinking of not only these souls, but of the millions of ancestors we were striving to remember through the Museum.

The chief had specific instructions for me.

Once the ancestors direct you to spill the soil over the wreck, he told me, *it will be the first time our people will have slept in their homeland. Bring them home. Look in their eyes*, he added. *We want you to deliver a message to our loved ones: that we have never forgotten.*

But he was not yet finished with me. It was just as important, he advised me, that these ancestors knew that they did, indeed, have descendants. To not have such progeny would be an unspeakable tragedy.

Do you see us? the chief demanded of me emphatically. He motioned to the other leaders who had joined us from their communities to encircle us. *Surely amongst the fallen,* the chief continued, *were those who were guardians of these same communities.* Pointing to them each in turn to let me know where they were from, he exhorted me: *Tell our ancestors that their people are still being cared for by those of us here before you.*

Visibly I remained composed (or at least, I think I did). Inside, I was overcome. The cowrie shell basket had become a symbol for all that the Museum was trying to do. The enormity of it hit me, and was both frightening and humbling.

We were no longer acting as initiators. We were now the vessel through which a part of history would move forward.

CLIFTON
SOUTH AFRICA, June 2, 2015

We left Mozambique as the São José had—with valuable cargo. Ours was of a different kind: the soil we had collected now stowed in Paul's suitcase, as precious as any artifact for the Museum we had carried. The soil had been transfigured into a physical testament to both those who had died and the land upon which those who had survived walked—into ancestor and descendant.

We would scatter this soil in Clifton, off of Cape Town, at the site of the wreck of the São José, so that the souls that were lost when the ship sank could rest in the familiar. We would not only honor these souls, but also commemorate all those whose destinies were altered by the slave trade.

ENCIRCLING

I have been to South Africa several times, helping to train museum and history professionals on interpreting important historical stories for the post-apartheid era. On a visit in 1997, I had met the great Nelson Mandela, who spoke of how he had drawn inspiration from our African American abolitionists— Frederick Douglass, Sojourner Truth, Harriet Tubman. Now we were in South Africa to remember the reason why America had had these courageous people.

To tighten the circle even more, we were gathering for a private ceremony in the home of Albie Sachs, the highly regarded anti-apartheid attorney whom Nelson Mandela had appointed as a judge in South Africa's newly democratized constitutional

court. Judge Sachs was blinded in his left eye and lost part of his right arm as the result of a bomb that was placed in his car when he was living in Mozambique in the 1980s.

Just a few weeks before our visit, several hundred Mozambicans had been deported from South Africa, in some ways a mirror to the five hundred who traveled on board the São José in 1794.

Our complicated journey was connecting past with present in unexpected ways.

FEBRUARY

We had expected that the moment when the soil was scattered to be dramatic. What I had not anticipated was how moving this small gathering beforehand, with Judge Sachs and his wife, Vanessa September, would be in their home near the beach.

Judge Sachs spoke passionately about the challenges in South Africa still today, and the ways in which stories like that of this shipwreck remained crucial for us to unearth and understand, no matter how painful. The judge had lived much of his life in the small waterfront community of Clifton. It was a place that had come to aptly serve as metaphor for our mission. In the water beneath the cove, a submerged slaver had languished for more than two centuries. Surrounding the cove now was a wealthy enclave of homes: a startling juxtaposition within a single community of the power of the recovered past to disturb the present.

Stela Brandão, a member of the Brazilian Consulate who had joined us, at one point began to sing a song of praise to the Orisha Yemanja, goddess of the sea. It was a completely spontaneous, unscripted response to Diana Ferrus's reading of the poem she had written to commemorate the occasion, her words connecting yesterday and today. A renowned South African poet, Diana has ancestors from Mozambique and feels a deep connection to the story of the São José. Her poem is called "My name is February," the title showing how those captured and enslaved were stripped of their own names and assigned the names of months as surnames.

Diana spoke in Afrikaans, Stela in Portuguese. I do not know either language, but it did not matter. Rather, it made me realize that we can help the world understand how global the slave trade was. A single vessel filled with near-sacred soil had brought together this highly diverse group of people. As all of us struggled to juxtapose the beauty of the site with the history of death, exploitation, slavery, and oppression submerged right off shore, and the legacy of apartheid in the city surrounding us, I was struck by how important it was to be bringing this powerful story back into memory. Depositing the soil in the water would create a giant ripple: a testimony to the truth that we cannot go backwards.

ANCESTORS

The water that day was so angry.

Ironically, the area where the slaver wrecked just three hundred twenty-eight feet from shore has become one of the most desirable places in Cape Town to live. On this day, however, the picturesque shoreline of Clifton was all but obliterated by the rain that was pouring down—more rain than I had ever seen in Cape Town. The sea was roiling, as if in pain. It was a day whose weather probably mirrored the day's the São José went down.

Steve and Jaco, whose diving had accorded them an intimate relationship with these waters, had determined that no boat could be sent upon the waves, nor diver under them. The trio tasked with delivering the earth entrusted to me by traditional leaders back in Mozambique would be able to approach it only by wading into the waves from the beach, taking care not to lose their footing in the agitated surf.

Just as anyone standing on shore that December day in 1794 could have witnessed the São José break up, we stood on the shore and watched as our three divers waded into the water, in what is known as the Cape of Storms, to get as close as they could to the site of the wreck.

The three carried the soil with them in the cowrie vessel—Kamau Sadiki, an African American searching for a connection to his ancestors; Tara Van Niekerk, a marine archaeologist from South Africa; and Yara de Larice, a college student from Mozambique. Each of their countries represented a part of the journey.

As the three scattered the soil into the sea and the enslaved who had perished here on December 27, 1794 were finally reconnected to their homeland, another unscripted, unexpected thing happened: the rain ceased, and the sun came out. I remembered what Paul had told me the year prior about his experience on the wreck site. *Never disrespect your ancestors*, I said to myself.

SANKOFA

It was as the chieftain in Mozambique had said: something more powerful than ourselves was using us. We had become the vessel.

It had been a journey. Surreal. Frightening. Wonderful.

We kept none of the soil we had brought from Mozambique, scattering all of it to the sea. We did keep the cowrie shell vessel, which is now in Washington at the Museum. Probably each of us who was there that day has kept something else as well.

For me, it's knowing that it wasn't soil inside those cowrie shells. It was souls. It was recalling the chieftain's admonition that this was no longer our idea: it was our ancestors'. It's being able now, every day, to dip into a reservoir of consecrated history, as if diving into that sea, and finding clarity, candor, and healing.

We have been made better by the strength and resilience of those who refused to let slavery strip them of their hopes and humanity. Only by grappling with the continuing resonance of slavery can we hope to create a global conversation that will help us find healing and peace.

It makes our job as a museum all the larger. We must be like Sankofa, the symbolic African bird that looks back to shape the present and the future. As a museum, we must be able not just to preserve the past but also to help a nation and a people move forward. In the United States in particular, slavery is one of the last great unmentionables in public discourse. As a national museum, it is essential that we help stimulate a national conversation on its impact, and an international dialogue.

RESCUE

We could not recover those who were lost in the wreck of the São José. But we could rescue their history. There is nothing more powerful than a people and a nation steeped in their history — all of it, both celebratory and tragic.

Through a far-reaching international collaboration — the Slave Wrecks Project, with the Iziko Museums of South Africa, The George Washington University, Diving With a Purpose, the African Centre for Heritage Activities, the South African Heritage Resource Agency, and the National Park Service in the United States — the Smithsonian is now able to bring this chapter of America's history closer to the millions who will visit our Museum.

No doubt there will be other books written on the journey of the São José, scholarly works that may nod to this one while they move the story forward. Before that happens and the moments are submerged in the historical record — the moment of discovery, the moment of first contact, the moment that the sun broke through — we wanted to capture those moments for you, the reader, and marvel at them, and remember.

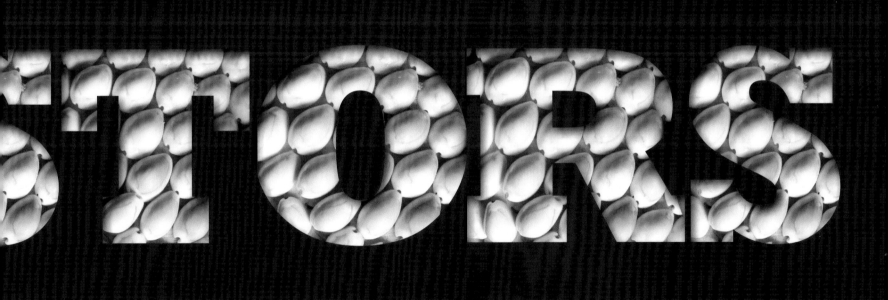

Number of years until soil from the captives' homeland was brought to the site of the shipwreck

A poem (in progress) **by Diana Ferrus
for the memorial tribute of the casualties
and survivors of the São José.**

My name is February

My naam is Februarie	*My name is February*
Ek is verkoop	*I was sold*
My borste, privaatdele, my oë	*my breasts, private parts and eyes*
my brein	*my brain*
is nog nie myne	*are not mine yet*
soos die Sao Jose	*like the São José*
loop ek opgekap	*I am ruined*
word ek telkens gesink deur 'n ander storm	*often sank by another storm*
geen Jesus wat op die water loop vir my	*no Jesus walking on water for me*
My naam is Februarie	*my name is February*
Ek soek nog die stang van die stuur	*I am searching for the rod of the steering wheel*
want onderwater le die familie	*because the family lies on the bottom*
die kind aan ma se rokspant	*the child stitched to mother's dress*
die ma aan pa se hand	*mother's hand locked in father's fist*
hoe diep lê hulle, aan watter kant	*how deep down are they lying, on which side*

My naam is Februarie
opgeveil, verkoop, die hoogste bieder
het ontslae geraak van my regte naam
geen vergoeding betaal
vir dit my naam, gesteel, gesink
onderwater lê dit nog
saam met die familie
wrakstukke van die Sao Jose
ten gronde geloop deur 'n wind
briesende branders wat die buit
se hele toekoms besluit
die profyt teen die wal uitsmyt

my naam is Februarie
die Masbieker op die Sao Jose
so was ek genoem
toe my hierse moedertaal gestalte kry
toe tonge met mekaar begin te knoop
en letters 'n vrye gang begin te loop
in 'n desperate poging in hoop
dat magte ook nie hierdie identiteit moet stroop
word ek die Masbieker, net 'n naam
onder 'n ander lug gekraam
en diep gevul met skaam

My naam is Februarie

my name is February
auctioned, sold, the highest bidder
disposed of my real name
paid no compensation
for that, my name, stolen, sunked
underwater it still lies
with the family
wrecks of the São José
ran aground by a wind
furious waves that decided
the future of the loot
smashing the profit against the embankment

my name is February
the Masbieker on the São José
that's how I was called
when my mother tongue of here came into being
when tongues started to form a bond
and letters started walking freely
in a desperate attempt at survival and hope
that forces should not strip this identity too
I became the Masbieker, only a name
born under a different sky
and deeply filled with shame

my name is February
I reshaped this landscape —
My hands wove the patterns of the vineyards
My feet pressed the grapes
and I was paid with the wine
I carry Alcohol-Foetal Syndrome children on my back

My name is February
I still march on the eve of December first
I walk the cobblestones of this city
when I cry in desperation
"remember the emancipation of the slaves!"

My name is February
two hundred years after the São José
I was given the vote
they said I was free

But do you see how often I am submerged
weighed down
I am the sunken, the soiled
forgotten
and yet memory will not leave me

My name is February
stranded at Third beach
but no one comes to look for me
no one waves from the dunes
no bridges back to Mozambique

my name is February
I will be resurrected
brought to the surface
unshackled, unchained, unashamed
My name is February.

THE WRITERS

The Authors

Jaco Jacqes Boshoff is Principal Archaeological Investigator for the excavation of the São José shipwreck and Maritime Archaeologist at Iziko, the confederation of national museums in Cape Town, South Africa, whose mission is to preserve and promote the diverse racial and cultural heritage of South Africa. "Iziko" is the isiXhosa word for "hearth"—the traditional center of a home, where stories are shared. Mr. Boshoff co-founded the Slave Wrecks Project in 2008 as the Southern African Slave Wrecks Project; Iziko is a core member.

Lonnie G. Bunch III is Founding Director of the National Museum of African American History and Culture, an appointment he accepted in 2005. In addition to his stewardship of the Museum's mission, exhibitions, and educational programs, he has established a program for members of the public to learn from museum conservators how to preserve family photos, papers, and objects of historical value to the African American experience. The former president of the Chicago Historical Society, Mr. Bunch has also served in various directorial capacities for the Smithsonian's National Museum of American History. He has taught at American University, his alma mater, as well as at the University of Massachusetts Dartmouth and The George Washington University. He is the author of the award-winning book *Call the Lost Dream Back: Essays on History, Race & Museums.* Mr. Bunch serves on the Commission for the Preservation of the White House by appointment by President Barack Obama.

Paul Gardullo is Museum Curator at the National Museum of African American History and Culture and serves as Co-Director of the Slave Wrecks Project. He played a lead role in conceptualizing, collecting for, and curating the Museum's inaugural exhibitions and overarching themes, including "The Power of Place" exhibition. Dr. Gardullo's work on the memory of slavery has appeared in special issues of the journals *Slavery and Abolition* and *Patterns of Prejudice.* He served on the editorial advisory board for the book *Smithsonian Civil War—Inside the National Collection.* Dr. Gardullo is the author of a book on slavery in American cultural memory (Oxford University Press; forthcoming).

Stephen C. Lubkemann is Associate Professor of Anthropology, Africana Studies, and International Affairs at The George Washington University in Washington, D.C., and is the Co-Principal Investigator in the archaeological and historical investigation of the São José story. A recipient of H.F. Guggenheim, Fulbright, and MacArthur fellowships, Dr. Lubkemann is also the co-founder of the GWU-Diaspora Research Program and a founding member of the GWU-Capitol Archaeological Institute. Trained in anthropology at Brown University, where he received his Ph.D., he has conducted extensive fieldwork as a cultural anthropologist and in historical archives in Mozambique, South Africa, Angola, and Liberia, and with African refugees and diasporas in Europe and the United States. He has also worked for more than two decades on projects in the field of maritime archaeology and heritage in Bermuda, the United States, Mozambique, and South Africa. In 2008, he co-founded and served as Coordinator of the Southern African Slave Wrecks Project, and now serves as the Slave Wrecks Project's International Coordinator and Co-Director. Dr. Lubkemann is the author of *Culture in Chaos: An Anthropology of the Social Condition in War.*

The Poet

Diana Ferrus is a South African writer, storyteller, and award-winning poet whose poetry on the complex issues of race and gender has garnered international acclaim. Her work, written in both Afrikaans and English, has been published in various collections, including texts for school curricula. She is the founder of an eponymous publishing house that has published the life stories of three South African activists in association with the University of the Western Cape, where she earned her postgraduate degree. Ms. Ferrus composed the poem "My naam is Februarie/My name is February" for the June 2, 2015 commemoration in Cape Town of the victims of the São José slave ship.

THE MUSEUM

The National Museum of African American History and Culture (NMAAHC) was created in 2003 by an Act of Congress, establishing it as part of the Smithsonian Institution. The Museum uses African American history and culture as a lens into what it means to be an American. It is also a place where all people will see how deeply connected African American history is not just to American but to world history, how our stories, histories, and cultures are shaped and informed by international considerations, and how the struggle of African Americans has impacted freedom struggles around the world.

NMAAHC is a place of collaboration, reaching beyond Washington to engage new audiences and to work with the myriad of museums and educational institutions, both nationally and internationally. Central to this collaborative role is the Museum's position as host to the Slave Wrecks Project, an international collaboration of institutions and researchers dedicated to advancing knowledge on understanding the global slave trade and its enduring legacies through research, training, education, and public engagement. Core members of the Slave Wrecks Project include The George Washington University, Iziko Museums of South Africa, and the U.S. National Park Service.

THE SYMBOL ⊕

This graphic, which appears throughout the book, is inspired by the Bakongo cross. A southwestern African icon, it has also been found in burial grounds, on earthenware vessels, and under dwellings in the Americas, where many captive Africans were enslaved. Its lines suggest a demarcation between the physical and spiritual worlds, while the circle surrounding them speaks to the cycle of life—birth, death, rebirth.

This symbol serves as an important metaphor for the Slave Wrecks Project. The Project literally and figuratively seeks to retrieve, resurface, and restore to memory that which has been lost and considered unknowable.

This project and the wider work of the Slave Wrecks Project worldwide could not have been accomplished without the people we acknowledge here. Their dedication, versatility, imagination, expertise, and good will make this expansive work possible, as do the myriad staff members, researchers, volunteers, and supporters who give so much to the Project.

The Slave Wrecks Project was conceived in conversations that began between friends and colleagues early in this century. At its core has always been an ethos of training, education, and deep community engagement to balance and inform the work of research and exploration. A special thank-you goes to our colleague, friend, and co-founder of the Slave Wrecks Project, Dr. David L. Conlin, for helping to bring this project to life from the very beginning.

Within the three institutions that created the Slave Wrecks Project, we have a number of people to thank.

At the Smithsonian Institution's National Museum of African American History and Culture
Staff, including Abby Benson, Nancy Bercaw, Nicole Bryner, Carlos Bustamante, James Early, Mary Elliot, Rex Ellis, John W. Franklin, Deborah Mack, Fleur Paysour, Klarissa Ruiz, Debora Scriber-Miller, Taima Smith, Kimberly Townsend, Ruthann Uithol, and Tsione Wolde-Michael.

At the Iziko Museums of South Africa
CEO Rooksana Omar and Executive Director of Core Functions Bongani Ndhlovu, together with Wayne Alexander, Albe Bosman, Nancy Childs, Wayne Florence, Shanaaz Gallant, Susan Glanville-Zini, Jake Harding, Melody Kleinsmith, Amy Sephton, Gerty Thirion, Paul Tichmann, and Ahmein Van der Walt.

At The George Washington University
Members of the Department of Anthropology, Africana Studies Program, Columbian School of Arts and Sciences, Elliot School of International Affairs, Diaspora Research Program, Institute for Ethnographic Research, Capitol Archaeological Institute, and Office of the Vice President for Research, along with Don Hawkins, Charles Maples, and deans Peg Barrat, Geralyn Schulz, and Ben Vinson.

In addition, we thank these institutions for their support: African Centre for Heritage Activities; Arquivo Histórico de Moçambique; Arquivo Histórico Ultramarino, Lisbon, Portugal; Association of the Friends of Mozambique Island; Central Analytical Facility, Stellenbosch University; Directorate of Cultural Patrimony of the Mozambique Ministry of Culture and Tourism; Diving With a Purpose; the Ford Foundation; Jason Martin and the Frog Squad; Eduardo Mondlane University, Department of Anthropology and Archaeology; Mozambique Ministry of Culture and Tourism; Smithsonian-GWU Opportunities Fund; South African Heritage Resources Agency; South African National Space Agency; Torre do Tombo, Lisbon, Portugal; United States Consulate, Cape Town, South Africa; United States Embassy, Maputo, Mozambique; University of Cape Town Biomedical Engineering; University of Witwatersrand Evolutionary Studies Institute; and Western Cape Archives.

Within the U.S. National Park Service, we thank in particular Biscayne National Park, Christiansted National Historic Site, Dry Tortugas National Park, Southeast Archaeological Center, and the Submerged Resources Center.

For those individuals who have contributed to the Project or the making of this book—or both—we thank Patrick Anderson, Marion Bamford, Reinaldo Barroso, Justine Benanty, Sean Berry, Michael Blakey, Jeremy Borelli, Jane Carpenter-Rock, Chenzira Davis-Kahina, Christopher DeCorse, Michelle Delaney, Yara de Larice, James Delgado, Adam Derstine, Andres Diaz, Ricardo Teixeira Duarte, Yolanda Teixeira Duarte, Anton Du Plessis, Diana Ferrus, Steve Gordon, John Gribble, Jay Haigler, Adair Hamilton, Meredith Hardy, Mim Harrison, Gaynelle Henderson, Bert Ho, Edward Howell, François Hugo, Hafiz Jamu, Jose Jones, Jessica Keller, Richard Kurin, Kristin Lamoreaux, Charles Lawson, Stefan Le Roux, Solange Macamo, Raquel Machaqueiro, Nicole Malli, Hilario Maquida, Harriet McGuire, Lalou Melzer, James A. Miller, Keneiloe

Molopyane, Alexandre Monteiro, Ray Moore, David Morgan, Decio Muianga, Diogo Oliveira, Susanna Pershern, Maia Puryear, Ciraj Rassool, Sean Reid, Aviva Rosenthal, Albie Sachs, Kamau Sadiki, George Schwarz, Vanessa September, Brett Seymour, Jonathan Sharfman, Michael Smith, Rick Sparkes, Tina St. Pierre, Stefan Steiner, Ken Stewart, Ibrahima Thiaw, Tara Van Niekerk, Heather Wares, Sophie Winton, and Jeneva Wright.

And finally, we thank our families for their love and undying support.

Jaco Jacqes Boshoff   **Lonnie G. Bunch III**
Paul Gardullo   **Stephen C. Lubkemann**

Illustration, Document and Photography Credits
Referenced by page number

Courtesy of Arquivo Histórico Ultramarino, Lisbon, Portugal

3 (right): Diagram. AHU-CU- 001 (Angola) Cx 79 Doc 67a.

3 (far right): Slaves Commodities. AHU-CU - 001 (Angola) Cx 81 Doc 4a.

33: Official list and crew of the ship St. Jose Paquete d'Africa from the city of Lisbon to Mozambique, 1794. AHU_CU 64 (MZ) CX 67 Doc 127.

40, 41: Report of the sale of a slave, 1794. AHU_CU 64 (MZ) CX 70 Doc 19.

47: Ship Manifest: Sao Jose Paquete d'Africa (Lisbon to Mozambique). AHU_CU 64 (MZ) CX 104 69 Doc Manifest.

62: Table dated 3 Sept. 1801, Mossambique, of ivory and other commodities.

Getty Images

89: Three divers scattering soil in the sea, Cape Town, South Africa. Image no. 475615606. Rodger Bosch/AFP/Getty Images.

Courtesy of Steve Gordon, cliftonpics.co.za: 84-85.

Courtesy of the Iziko Museums of South Africa

Facing half-title: "Table Bay Cape Town" oil on panel by Thomas Luny (1759-1837). Photograph by Pam Warne.

49 (scan): Central Analytical Facilities, University of Stellenbosch.

Courtesy of the National Archives of the Netherlands

28-29: 15., Collectie C. J. van de Graaff. TOPO 15, Kaarten en tekeningen betreffende Kaap de Goede Hoop, Ceylon en Malakka. 1687-1801. 15.55, Kaart van de Baay van Cams over het gebergte aan de Kloof ten noorden van de Caap de Goede Hoop ... door den Ingenieur Barbier, minuut. (A264). 1788 1 blad.

Courtesy of Kamau Sadiki: 81.

Shutterstock

76: mokokomo/Shutterstock.com.

Courtesy of the Slave Wrecks Project. © Smithsonian National Museum of African American History and Culture, Iziko Museums of South Africa and The George Washington University

Facing title page, 27: Photographs by Jason Martin.

xiv, 1, 5, 8, 16 (pulley), 44, 49 (image), 50-51, 58, 63: Photographs by Dreamcatcher Productions.

9, 12, 24, 36, 43, 52, 67: Photographs by Jonathan Sharfman.

Smithsonian National Museum of African American History and Culture

75, 77, 79 (sign), 82-83: Photographs by Paul Gardullo.

79 (ramp): Photograph by Carlos Bustamante.

Collections of the Smithsonian National Museum of African American History and Culture:

72, 91, 99.

Courtesy of the United States National Park Service

16 (underwater shot), 18-19, 61: Photographs by Susanna Pershern.

Courtesy of The Western Cape Archives and Records Service, Document NCD 2/18, no 299 ¼

56, 57: Pages from the deposition of the captain of the São José.

NORTH AMERICA

ATLANTIC OCEAN

SOUTH AMERICA

Maranhão
Brazil

The Path
of the São José 1794